THE

MODERN DANCE TECHNIQUE

THE

MODERN DANCE TECHNIQUE

by **Renata Celichowska**

Illustrations by Leon Belokon

Labanotation by Ilene Fox

Princeton Book Company, Publishers

This project was made possible by a grant from the National Initiative to Preserve America's Dance (NIPAD), a program under the umbrella SAVE AS: DANCE, underwritten by The Pew Charitable Trusts and administered at Dance/USA.

A Dance Horizons Book
Princeton Book Company, Publishers
P.O. Box 831
Hightstown, NJ 08520

Interior and cover design by Ben Hillman
Composition by Doric Lay Publishers

Library of Congress Cataloging-in-Publication Data
Celichowska, Renata.
  The Erick Hawkins modern dance technique / by Renata Celichowska ;
illustrations by Leon Belokon ; labanotation by Ilene Fox.
      p. cm.
  Includes bibliographical references (p.) and index.
  ISBN 0-87127-213-X
      1. Hawkins, Erick—Philosophy.   2. Modern dance—Philosophy.
I. Hawkins, Erick.   II. Title.
GV1783 .C39 2000
792.8—dc21
                                                                                00-044091

Printed in Canada

To Erick, with Love

There's no shortcut

about learning dancing.

You just have to get in there,

and step by step,

see how the thing feels. . . .

— Erick Hawkins

Erick Hawkins in *Early Floating*, 1961.

CONTENTS

ILLUSTRATIONS

PHOTOGRAPHS

LABANOTATION*

*See pages 161–64 for information about the Labanotation process and reading Labanotation.

ACKNOWLEDGMENTS

There are so many people in the Hawkins world whom I respect and admire that it is difficult to know how to adequately recognize them all. Erick's legacy has sprouted many beautiful branches with many blossoms.

Nada Diachenko will always stay in my heart as the person who first showed me this world, and for that I am eternally grateful.

I continue to learn from the amazing people in the company with whom I danced and studied, including Douglas Andresen, Beverly Brown, Brenda Connors, Katherine Duke, Kelly Holt, Randy Howard, Gloria McLean, Nancy Meehan, Michael Moses, Kathy Ortiz, Laura Pettibone Wright, James Reedy, Cynthia Reynolds, Frank Roth, Sean Russo, Daniel Tai, Mariko Tanabe, Catherine Tharin, Cathy Ward, Lillo Way and Robert Yohn. They have all been a wonderful source of inspiration for me over the years and have helped make this book as accurate and objective a resource as possible.

A special thanks to Cynthia Reynolds for helping me keep a sense of myself through all of these years and to Katherine Duke for keeping me laughing. Together with unfailing support from Bud Baker and Tad and Susan Crawford, Robert Engstrom has been the backbone of this project. Thank you Bob, Bud, Tad and Susan for your advice and encouragement. The project would not have been possible without you.

A personal thanks to Andrea Snyder and Greg Ruffer of the National Initiative to Preserve America's Dance (NIPAD), to Ilene Fox of the Dance Notation Bureau, to Ben Hillman and Leon Belokon of Ben Hillman & Company, and to Charles Woodford and Karen Deaver of Princeton Book Company, Publishers, for their belief in this project.

Endless thanks to Nadra Holmes, whose energy and expertise on the video portion of this project realized itself in a beautiful work.

Of course, love and thanks to Lucia Dlugoszewski, whose untamed spirit and passion for art will continue to sing to me.

Love to my family and friends, who always support me through my various adventures. You are the reason I keep going. Thank you Krystyna, Stefan, Ewa, Misia, John, Charlie, Alex, Stefan, Julia, Deb and Patti. I love you all.

And, most importantly, thanks to Erick for changing my life and giving me back my dancing. I miss you.

Renata Celichowska
January 2000

TRIBUTE

Purity and innocence are the parameters of a delicacy of spirit that evokes Erick Hawkins. No other artist has ever been singled out this way, unless perhaps Dante.

Like Dante, Erick was not afraid to embrace elegance and beauty or the mythic grandeur of the human condition. Whether he approached technique or choreography, whether his originality veered into the philosophic, the aesthetic or the poetic or just the sheer fun of being alive, he was always on an adventure.

A New Dance Technique

Erick's breakthrough vision of singling out and putting a laserlike focus on the front muscles of the legs and torso, making them the sole source of control in initiating movement in all the other muscles of the body, was a great intuitive insight into technique.

It generated an animal essence of extraordinary sensuousness in the performances of his dancers. It also brought a special capacity for passion, as is found in the bullfighters he so admired, and a kind of dazzling efficiency one finds in the Shaker furniture he so adored.

Unlike other great modern dance initiators who approach technique through the idiosyncratic force of their own personal egos, Erick was constantly in pursuit of a selfless, generic wisdom that grasps the whole, comprehensive spectrum of movement and its holistic power.

For several years, when important artists died the greatest accolade seemed to be to link them with Picasso or James Joyce. Erick Hawkins certainly matched that Spaniard and that Irishman with his own prodigious creativity and originality of large vision; but Erick had an even larger gift. He had the keenest poetic grasp of reality of any artist I can think of.

He radically redefined choreography as a primal poetic experience that resulted in something new that was concrete rather than abstract; something beyond metaphor and symbol.

He was truly able to reclaim an uncompromising purity of the concrete, bringing about a one-man revolution in the art form of dance.

Even in Erick's first choreography, called *Showpiece* (1937), there were already elements of his unique kind of "pure movement." George Balanchine praised it as the most original effort of that year's Ballet Caravan repertory. It was his emerging poetic "concreteness" that made up the originality that Balanchine spotted.

Erick's feeling for the poetically "concrete" also affected the significant contribution he made to Martha Graham's work. He brought to Graham's choreography the mythic Greek root for expressing the human condition in an epic mode. He totally revolutionized partnering in "concretely" poetic terms. He created a new kind of passion between a man and woman onstage, balancing symbolism and reality like a fine edge of Toledo steel.

An American Original

Perhaps Erick was so often called the quintessential American artist because he imitated no one. His mind was his own.

Erick did not derive from anywhere. With each new work, he invented and reinvented himself in the stark solitude of himself by himself. It was only after he forged his fascinating dance technique that he encountered Aikido.

It was only after he launched his outrageous poetic structures that he found corroboration in Far Eastern classical poetry. It was only after he created the ferocity of his inexplicably leaping dynamics that he discovered a similar nonlinear creative power in Zen Buddhism.

His so-called influences, whether Zen, Greek or Southwest Indian, were much more of a sharing with kindred spirits and the relief from the scary loneliness of being so ahead of his time than the driving force of an outer inspiration.

There was nothing "neo" about him. He was for real!

The Anti-naïve "Realistic" Revolution

Erick Hawkins was the only artist to really understand the devitalizing effect of naïve realism.

His nonlinearness and his strangeness that puzzled so many were also his greatest gifts of all, fierce tools to secure the bedrock core of poetic immediacy.

Perhaps what made him one of the most original choreographic voices of our time was the ferociously continuing commitment to the destroying of naïve realistic literalness. He demolished all of those dead, fixed, conventional, safe and literal meanings to strangely renew the very act of experience itself, or to dangerously restore to existence the quality of adventure.

In a time of claustrophobic technological takeovers of our lives, when the belief in authenticity of personal experiences is increasingly called into question, where experience itself and spiritual connections with the real world are often lost, jettisoned or forgotten, Erick created one wild, revolutionary red sleeve in a dance and produced the strangest nonlinear work in the world about a pine tree. In one stroke he annihilated the deadness of naïve realism forever. One outrageously disparate red sleeve suddenly redefined a whole new way of looking at dance.

He was genuinely a strange man, this quintessential American. He was a nonlinear genius, a Melville and a Thoreau at the same time; only the Far Eastern classical poets had the capacity for such inspired strangeness.

In this radically new style of dance, he was the playfulness of Zen and the heaviness of the Spanish "duende."[*]

The Zen of Hawkins and the Hawkins of Zen

There exists not only a Zen paradox of Japanese spiritual refinement, there is also the Erick Hawkins paradox: a radical poetic refinement that is something very American, by an American in the best sense of the word.

A lot of Erick's originality revolves around his penchant for the fertilizing disturbance of dichotomies that so fascinated him — his predilection for ferociously delicate balances between opposites, securing in his own way a deeper Zen glimpse into the real world.[†]

The Activist

Does the concrete purity of his choreography fit the twenty-first century, thrust as we are into the activist and socially critical passion of our troubled times? Yes, it does, but in an important way that eludes the perception of many.

Not only was he never afraid of beauty, his unique choreographic risk

[*] For a further understanding of "duende," refer to the essays of Spanish author Federico Garcia Lorca.
[†] For further information on the Zen influences on both Hawkins and Dlugoszewski, see the writings of Shunryu Suzuki listed under Recommended Reading.

was to put beauty and rage in the same dangerous equation. This made his *Ahab*, his *Killer of Enemies*, his *God the Reveller* so glorious for some and so difficult for others.

He challenged our credibility in a fascinating way by speaking violence and elegance in the same breath. This is what was finally called his "violent clarity."

He really was the first activist choreographer with *John Brown* (1947), before a lot of people even thought about those issues, but he never succumbed to the activist need for naïvely realistic, linear expression.

Like Thoreau, this strangely unique artist was committed most fiercely to civil liberties, while in the same breath he celebrated the delicate power of a flower.

Stepping Over All Boundaries

He really was a multifaceted kind of Renaissance man. We are just beginning to understand the enormity and importance of his influence on his time. Whenever one considers the primal essentials of what is dance—time, space, dynamics, metaphor, energy—his revolution is felt in every corner of the art.

Space Adventure

He was the first to explore the asymmetrical use of space and time.

By intensely redefining every inch of the dancing space in taut, poetic terms, he actually sensualized space.

Time Adventure

He was particularly special about time. His new time sense was the fiercest experience of creative immediacy of which I know.

No one has quite matched his knife's edge force of contemplation onstage.

He was capable of arresting time, of tilting it in all directions of speed and stillness. The incredible way he used the paradox of leaps between utter speed and unspeakable stillness released a new kind of energy.

He stretched or distilled duration carefully and deeply, brushing the cutting edges of a new time experience.

This new kind of time involved not exterior silence but interior silence, a stunning athleticism from within.

Metaphor: The "Disparate Elements" Revolt

When Far Eastern poetic geniuses, like Bashō, Buson and Shiki, wanted to elicit the purest, most uncompromising poetic response, their strategy was to "fling into" the situation a total non sequitur as a mystical "something" to stimulate the mind into a sense of wonder through the disturbing presence of strangeness. They called this "something" the "disparate" element.

No one ever pushed the sense of the disparate to bolder refinement than Erick Hawkins, not even the classical poets from the Far East.

He set aside the predictable linear symmetry of metaphor and replaced it with the life-giving surprise of the inexplicable. Thus, the Hawkins disparate adventure began.

Why, indeed, do two women in narrow black robes strangely throw white tissue paper up in the air and catch it on the way down in his dance "Moon and Clouds" from *Black Lake*?

Nature and the "Disparate Element"

Someone once compared the genius of Hawkins with the genius of Blake — the disturbing energy and subtlety of nature in both; the élan and vibrancy of poetic causality at work.

Someone else spoke of *Black Lake* as coming very close to the selfless identification with nature that predates most religions.

Every one of the eight dances in the *Black Lake* vision are audacities of metaphors that are "disparately beyond metaphor." They come from deep within, dazzling the eye and challenging the mind: the night sky as a sequence of eight privileged visions.

This stands as a Hawkins testament to his revolutionizing reality beyond metaphor, which has a new impact on all the arts — this disparate tightrope on which he is the Olympian athlete.

Because of this, no choreographer has been more powerful in capturing the ungraspable grandeur of nature than Erick Hawkins.

In Hawkins' dances nature is distilled and monumentalized in daring dimensions even surpassing his beloved risk-taking Eastern poets.

Dynamics Breakthrough

Perhaps the most provocative, the most original, the most compelling and perhaps the most misunderstood of Erick's explorations involve dynamics.

His fundamental revolution in dynamics elicits a heightened, almost ragelike immediacy onstage that rivets the consciousness.

Dynamics was his most special discovery — a thrilling, perilous momentum deriving from the abrupt cliff-hanging shifts and leaps in levels of kinesthetic energy.

It is exciting because it does not wipe out the essential danger of dance. The special essence of his originality and dynamics is that strange risk of moving — those mercurial dislocations that are the coming face-to-face with the unexpected.

Passion

In the early years of Erick's technical discoveries, dancers came to study his philosophies of movement training and meditation often to heal themselves in both body and soul. At that time, as it was always, Erick's choreography explored fierce poetic adventures, but he was careful not to disturb anyone's physical fragility.

This emphasis created an erroneous limiting perception of Erick's work, viewed as something merely gentle and beautiful and quiet, but somehow lacking in dynamic excitement and strength. By the late 1970s, a wide range of students began to flock to his classes, including virtuosic professionals, and his choreography was able to explore different facets of his technical vision, including more adventurous physicality. The beautiful, the gentle and the quiet still evoked their strange and haunting power over his work, but he was able to train his dancers to fulfill another deep need of his, the expression of passion. In 1988 he created *Cantilever II*.

Suddenly the originality of his technique was given free play in the bold liberation of the body. The revolutionary use of fluidity, and a new largeness and translucence made possible by passion — something so wild, so untested, so mysterious — was a direct change of consciousness in the way the body moves.

Here was a fierceness of dynamics that was unique in choreography and truly demonstrated the full, reckless rage of a radically new style of dance.

Cantilever II became a strange masterpiece of dynamic structuring, an architecture of dangerous beauty with sudden, kinesthetic power shifts.

Who Is Erick Hawkins?

Because of his startling methodology with the use of the disparate element, some Hawkins admirers say metaphor is his supreme achievement. Actually, it is something new replacing conventional metaphor.

Still others say his revolution is yet to be understood. Maybe that is why young people continue to be interested in him.

Only recently someone said Erick is still making what he once called "a pure act of movement a thing of wonder," and someone else said of him that he choreographed like a very young man.

He has been called one of America's greatest geniuses. He has also been called a maverick and a wild man and a fool.

In Hong Kong they wrote, "Caution: Radical Master at Work."

In California they said, "His genius is for free flight."

Erick never stopped the adventure of his life. He finished choreographing *Journey of a Poet* for Mikhail Baryshnikov the day before he died. He completed *The Last Love Duet* and *Why Does a Man Dance?* a month before he died.

He is now the Future. And it is still being written.

F.S.C. Northrop called him "one of the greatest artists working in any field that our time has produced."

But for me there was something else: something intensely moving in his vulnerability, something utterly poetic in his moments of supreme risk.

The Vulnerable Body

When I first met Erick Hawkins I had never been up close to a dancer, especially a male dancer. I came to my first rehearsal with him and he met me barechested, dressed only in tights. I had also never before had the opportunity of watching a dancer moving up close and I certainly never before saw such a man. Every male bare torso that I had ever known had a kind of armored hardness of muscle across the chest. Not only was Erick's body truly like one of his beloved archaic Greek sculptures, there was also an added uniqueness. In addition to all of his muscular strength, his pectorals, his abdomenal muscles, he had an added delicate sensibility derived from the technical originality of his vision. There was no other way to describe his chest except in terms of incredible vulnerability, an expressive physicality of tenderness that I never expected a man to possess. Even a simple opening of the arms to someone became what was documented as his tender gesture in all of his incomparable love dances.

No one, not the Greek, not D.H. Lawrence, not Isadora Duncan had a greater love for the sensuous, gentle, naked, moving human body than Erick Hawkins.

Collaboration

Marie von Frantz'[‡] archetype of the creative process is of jumping unsupported through the center of a ring. Erick Hawkins, more than anyone I have ever known, was this person who jumped.

His greatest choreographic pleasure was a heart-stopping leap into the unknown.

Sometimes I jumped after him.

Sometimes we used to hold each other's hands and jump together at the same time.

That could maybe describe our collaboration.

My Personal Life with Erick Hawkins

Someone who really loved our work together called us a cloudless collaboration. Actually, we were both almost dangerously independent. That made for some passionate interchanges.

But it is true, when we first met we thrilled over the fact that in our very different ways we were both already practicing our individual crusade against the stultifying effects of naïvely realistic art and we each obsessed in our own original manners about the beauty of disparate elements. He used to love to tease me by saying, "You were made in heaven to write the music for the 'Pine Tree.'"

[‡]Marie von Frantz was psychologist Carl Jung's most significant collaborator.

Aesthetically, Erick and I especially "collaborated" in being at least as passionately transfixed as were the haiku poets by the beauty of the natural world. We really went to great lengths to achieve this "collaboration."

Close to where Erick was born there is one of those Navajo sacred places that they love so intensely: a huge natural rock "sculpture" they call "Agathlon." We also shared a love for this beautiful "Agathlon" as we lay in a sleeping bag together at the foot of such a sculpture and watched this rock calibrate a moonrise with strange, careful magic. We slept here every time we camped in Indian country during those years.

Women are always asking men if they love them, and Erick's answer to such a question was "I love you the way I love to look at the beauty of Agathlon."

In the 1970s Erick first rented the apartment at 15 East Eleventh Street and took me there at night to show me where another full moon was turning the empty room into incredible hugeness. "I especially chose this place so I could show you this moon whenever I felt like it and we could lie here and love it together."

In October 1994, when we came back from the White House, where he received the President's Medal for the Arts from President Clinton, Erick suddenly had a period of a lot of reminiscing. He once said to me, "Do you remember when I first met you and decided to take you to Nantucket to seduce you, and we were walking along the beach at night and I took your hand and said, 'I never want to give up this hand,' and here I am still holding this hand."

Erick and I were married September 1, 1962, in my mother's garden in Waterford Township, Michigan, by Lake Elizabeth.

Because of professional choice, it was only after 1994 that I for the first time publicly faced the world as Erick's wife, and as such I would like to say:

He was the most beautiful man I ever knew. He was the sexiest man I ever knew.

He was the most gloriously reckless man I ever knew, in his work, in his mind, in his heart.

And I loved him more than my own life.

Erick was a little fascinated by my Polishness, maybe because Poland treasures her male dancers the way America treasures her basketball stars.

He especially loved a little Polish song that I often sang for him about the Mazurka dancer named Maciek, who died and yet still jumped up to dance because this was what it is to have the spirit of the Mazur.

I celebrate Erick with this song.

Maciek has died.
He has died.
And he is lying on a board.
Maciek has died but something strange is happening.
For in a Mazur there is such a spirit
That even when he is lying dead he jumps up dancing.

Lucia Dlugoszewski
January 2000

I. HISTORICAL BACKGROUND

Nothing is ever separated from any other relationship in the world . . . how we dance stems from our total philosophic view of our human life and, insofar as our philosophic idea is partial or has gaps in it, our dance can be stiffened or set, become limited or only partially functioning. The body is not divided from the mind, the soul.

In this sense, it seems to me that what you might call the mental world or the spiritual world has an exact analogy in training of the body. The way of tight muscles, tension, strain, violence, force and aggressiveness in the body registers the analogous state of the soul.

If the dance is to be of excellence and vitality, and if it is to be a metaphor of our existence, then we have to consider what good existence is, or even what existence is, period. So my conclusion is, if you want to arrive at quality, at real excitement and real intensity in the art of dance, you have to look at real quality in existence.[1]

[1] Erick Hawkins, interview by Gail Myers, unpublished videotape, Texas, 1979.

These are the words of American modern dance master Erick Hawkins, an artist who over the span of his sixty-year career in dance lived to manifest a profound integration of body, mind and soul through his art. Based upon this simple premise, Hawkins wove a sophisticated fabric of interconnected ideas that is one of the most comprehensive and cohesive philosophies of dance to emerge out of the twentieth-century modern dance movement.

In a Western world where faster, bigger and stronger was, and still is, a driving force, Hawkins, beginning in the 1950s, became a "maverick"[2] of a reverse aesthetic: one of grace, sensuousness, immediacy, poetry and free, effortless flow. In a 1982 interview, Hawkins described how his life experiences lead him to explore a way of merging the aesthetic ideas of the East with the logical movement theories of the West:

> Through my own injuries I began to see what the science of kinesiology was finding out about movement and dance technique. And I began to see that there was something rotten in the State of Denmark in the Western idea about dance training and its attitude toward the body. . . . So, I began to see that we could not have a new dance in America if we based our movement on anything that violated science.
>
> . . . the next step of my development, I would say, was the coupling of the metaphysical and aesthetic ideas from the Orient with our Western kinesiological science.
>
> Our Western idea has always been that you have to discipline the body and work hard. I saw that we badly needed the complementary idea, say from Chinese philosophy, of the balance of the opposites of the Yin and

---

[2] *New York Times* dance critic Anna Kisselgoff named Hawkins a "maverick" of the modern dance in a 1980 article for *Harvard* magazine, May–June 1980. It was a description that Hawkins relished in reference to his work.

the Yang, the balance of doing and not doing. Now the
joke of it is that the idea of doing and not doing is
exactly the way that you move the muscles and move the
bones. And so, it [Chinese philosophic thought] was
totally scientific. But it was not arrived at by science.
It was arrived at by the intuition, by immediate appre-
hension and *that* is, then, Eternal.[3]

It is this unwavering belief in the ultimate worth of merging Eastern
aesthetic intuition with Western science that sets Hawkins apart from his
contemporaries. Considered somewhat of an iconoclast and a rebel during his career, he had the conviction and courage to follow and champion
this unique aesthetic.

Hawkins was a maverick from the first. The son of an inventor, he
was born and raised in Trinidad, Colorado, and later lived with his family
in St. Louis, Missouri, before moving east to attend Harvard. Hawkins
was first introduced to dance as an art form in 1930, when he saw a performance given by the dance artists Yvonne Georgi and Harald Kreutzberg in New York City.

Well, once I got to see a performance in New York
of two German dancers, Kreutzberg and Georgi. Right
away from the first intermission I knew it was what I
wanted to do . . . and I had literally never heard that
there was such a thing as dancing upon the stage before.[4]

At the time of the Kreutzberg concert, Hawkins was still a Harvard
student, studying classical literature and culture. The accomplished
artistry and masculine energy of Kreutzberg's dancing deeply affected

[3] Erick Hawkins, Gail Myers interview.
[4] Ibid. Harald Kreutzberg, a disciple of Mary Wigman, successfully combined his strong ballet background with
Wigman's weighted German expressionist technique. His tours to the United States during the late 1920s and early
1930s inspired many male dancers throughout America, including José Limón and Hawkins.

Hawkins. Upon completing his final year at Harvard, he participated in a summer dance workshop with Kreutzberg in Austria, after which he decided to move to New York City to pursue further training.

During this first year in New York, Hawkins found himself still questioning dance's role in his life. The following summer, he took an extended trip to visit the native American Pueblo and Plains Indian tribes near the place of his birth and childhood in Trinidad. He described the thoughts he had during that summer:

> After I had started my first dance training, for two years I did not write to my family to tell them what I was doing. When a young man has arrived at his vocation and is put in the terrible position that his vocation in the world's eyes is a questionable one for a man, you can see what trouble he is in.
>
> After a couple of more years of training, I took a summer off to settle this question for myself. I was born on the New Mexico–Colorado line, very close to the oldest dance cultures in America: Those of the Seven Cities of Cibola, the Zuni, the Rio Grande Pueblos, the Hopis and Navajos. But I had never seen any of their dance ceremonies. So I spent the summer traveling around in an old Model A Ford, ferreting out word of every dance given that summer in New Mexico and Arizona. I had to see and feel whether a grown man could dance without being a fool.
>
> That was a wonderful summer for me, for it set my soul at rest. . . . That summer told me that I had seen men use dance as part of their worship, part of their way of coming into harmony with their own life and the lives of all the other centers of the world around them. . . .
>
> That summer made me know that I would never be happy until I found a way to make dance for all Ameri-

Erick Hawkins in Union Square, New York City, c. 1950.

cans part of a concept of totality. I knew that dance
would never be, for me, only entertainment.[5]

Having found affirmation of his belief in the beauty and power of
dance during this trip, Hawkins returned east to continue his formal
dance training.

From 1934 to 1938, Hawkins studied at the fledgling School of
American Ballet, begun by George Balanchine and Lincoln Kirstein.
During his years with Balanchine, Hawkins became involved in all
aspects of dance: He was exposed to Balanchine's choreographic and
musical genius while watching and participating in rehearsals; he became
the first student to begin teaching at Balanchine's school; and from 1936
to 1938, he danced and choreographed as a company member of
Kirstein's Ballet Caravan.[6]

Although aesthetic differences later drew Hawkins away from

[5] Erick Hawkins, *The Body Is a Clear Place*, Princeton Book Company, Publishers, Princeton, 1992, pp. 55–56.
[6] Anatole Chujoy, *The New York City Ballet: The First Twenty Years*, Da Capo Press, New York, 1982.

Balanchine's world, Hawkins' training with Balanchine provided an excellent introduction to dance technique and the challenges of the choreographic process. Throughout his career, Hawkins frequently mentioned his admiration for Balanchine's creative genius in weaving dance and music together and for his unquestionable commitment to his artistic vision.

Among the ideas that began to interest Hawkins more was the search for a uniquely "American" dance aesthetic, expressed through a new movement vocabulary. In his characteristically outspoken style, Hawkins once described his feelings on the subject:

> When I first started getting into the dance, I began
> to see that if I was going to have any fun, I needed to see
> what I could find out. The idea of just regurgitating
> what had been done in dear old Russia was nauseating![7]

In July of 1936, Ballet Caravan made its debut at Bennington College, sharing concert space with American modern dancer Martha Graham and her company. Graham's work immediately spoke to a kindred "American" spirit in Hawkins and he quickly became interested in developing his dancing in this direction.

At the suggestion of Muriel Stuart, one of Hawkins' influential teachers at Balanchine's school, Hawkins began studying at the Graham school, and soon thereafter began to attend rehearsals with Graham and her company.

During the ensuing twelve-year affiliation (1938–1950) with Martha Graham, Hawkins and Graham shared an intense and powerful personal and artistic relationship. In 1938, Hawkins became the first male dancer to join the Graham troupe, appearing in *American Document*. He later

---

[7] Erick Hawkins, Gail Myers interview.

Erick Hawkins and Martha Graham in Bennington, Vermont, 1940.

© BARBARA MORGAN

Martha Graham, Erick Hawkins and Merce Cunningham in *El Penitente*, Bennington, Vermont, 1940.

created the lead male roles for *Every Soul Is a Circus* (1939), *El Penitente* (1940), *Letter to the World* (1940), *Punch and the Judy* (1941), *Deaths and Entrances* (1943), *Appalachian Spring* (1944), *Dark Meadow* (1946), *Cave of the Heart* (1946), *Night Journey* (1947) and *Eye of Anguish* (1950).

The complete commitment to their art form was a prevalent characteristic of both Graham and Hawkins as artists. Hawkins often related an observation he made while performing with Graham in *Appalachian Spring*. It struck Hawkins how intently Graham experienced each moment of the piece, whether she was moving or standing still. This total involvement with the performing moment became a lasting influence for Hawkins.

Hawkins and Graham shared many other similar ideas on art and dance. They were both advocates of developing an authentic American dance heritage, and both were committed to the idea of "total" theater.[8] Hawkins' passion for Greek and classic literature kindled Graham's imagination and became the basis for some of Graham's most powerful works, such as *Night Journey* (1947), *Errand into the Maze* (1947) and *Clytemnestra* (1958). Hawkins' love of Greek classicism is evident in such pieces as his *openings of the (eye)* (1952), *Greek Dreams, with Flute* (1973), *Meditations on Orpheus* (1974) and *God the Reveller* (1987).

Despite these common interests, by the late 1940s artistic and personal differences began to pull the two artists apart. One of the primary differences between Graham and Hawkins, as Hawkins described it, was that Graham's artistic approach and technical theories stressed an obvious "willfulness" of the body, which became increasingly fraught with tension. This tension in the body began to register for Hawkins an equal tension in the mind and soul.

> It soon became evident to me that strain in the body asked for strain in the soul or psyche, or whatever we call the inward man. As I grew up I saw evidences that spiritual enlightenment, or whatever else you want to call it, has its analogy in the grace of the body. The goal of all spiritual leaders is to avoid strain. They want harmony in all kinds of moral and physical areas. The goal is to avoid strain on any level of activity: mental or physical, personal or political and cultural.
>
> If the soul is deeply at peace, if the person is wholly at one with itself, full of wonder, full of love, it will not have to shoot the arrow. It will know how in confidence, joy and self-knowledge to let the arrow shoot itself.[9]

[8] The term "total" is used in reference to the full design of all aspects of the theater: proscenium stage, costumes, lighting, stage properties, music, etc. All of these theatrical devices, even if consciously omitted, are very much a part of both Graham's and Hawkins' artistic work.
[9] Hawkins, *The Body Is a Clear Place*, p. 97. This reference to "letting the arrow shoot itself" is based upon Zen ideas presented in Eugen Herrigel's *Zen in the Art of Archery*.

From his years of training, first as a ballet dancer at Balanchine's school, then as a modern dancer with Graham, Hawkins was aware of the constant manipulation of the body away from its natural or "normative" beauty.[10] This distortion began to feel and look increasingly unappealing to him. For him, the sensitivity and suppleness of the human spirit were being sacrificed to achieve an unnatural ideal. In this sense, Hawkins' initial investigations in dance training were the result of a desire to find the physical equivalent of man's most beautiful spiritual and emotional life:

> What originally motivated me to discover a new body discipline was the desire to train the body to a responsiveness that would express that essential delight of men and women together and all the wonderful psychological implications that the success of such a union implies. I could not find an existing body vocabulary that could satisfy my vision. Existing dance vocabulary struck me as cold, insipid, unresponsive, or aggressive and unyielding.[11]

After years of his own investigations, Hawkins discovered for himself that:

> Beautiful dancing is then, finally, always about love, told with love, which is the most heightened perception, with effortless, free flowing muscles that can both feel and love.[12]

This idea of expressing a "heightened perception" through dance became one of Hawkins' primary goals as an artist. In Eastern aesthetics, such as in haiku poetry, Chinese brush painting and Japanese Noh the-

[10] For further explanation of the term "normative," see "The Normative Ideal" in chapter II.
[11] Hawkins, *The Body Is a Clear Place*, p. 82.
[12] Ibid, p. 77.

BILL AND GWEN SLOAN

Beautiful dancing is then, finally, always about love. Erick Hawkins and Barbara Tucker in *here and now, with watchers*, c. 1960.

ater, Hawkins found a similar emphasis on reawakening perception and sensory experience. He saw that staying alive in the moment of existence was a way of heightening life's experience:

> It's as if the whole endeavor of our life — and certainly that of being an artist — is to bring everything to consciousness. . . .
> . . . all wise people have tried to arrive at how to stay in one's own skin and bones. All the way from Jesus who said "Do not be anxious about tomorrow. . . . Consider the lilies of the field, how they grow; they neither toil nor spin. . . . Even Solomon in all his glory was not arrayed like one of these."[13]

[13] Matthew 6: 25–29.

And to be able to actually see the experience of the outer world without profit or loss is probably one of the most difficult things to do for the human being, with his egotistical pretentiousness and his own egotistical needs.

But, as we learn to stay in the pleasure and the refreshment of art . . . gradually, maybe philosophically, we will learn the idea of a wonderful Japanese man who once said, 200 years ago, "The natural state of man's mind is delight."[14]

In searching for a way to "bring everything to consciousness," Hawkins desired to regain sensation in the body and share this physical experience with the audience. The word "coenesthesia" means a "commonly felt state of sensation" ("coen," meaning common, and "esthesia," meaning feeling).[15] When a dancer becomes attuned to his or her coenesthetic sense it means that he or she is actively experiencing movement through the senses. The weight of the leg swinging through a loop, the sensation of a breeze brushing past the face and arms, the rhythm that the body sings in response to music, the colors and shapes around the dancer: A dancer truly experiencing such sensations shares these experiences with the observer more viscerally and effectively.

With the instinct and desire to search for a way in which to incorporate ideas of releasing excess tension, of experiencing a heightened immediacy in movement and a reawakened coenesthetic sense of movement, in 1950 Erick Hawkins left Graham and the Graham Company.

---

[14] Erick Hawkins, Gail Myers interview. Quote from Toju Nakae.

[15] Hubert Benoit, *The Supreme Doctrine*, Inner Traditions International, Ltd., New York, 1984. "Coenesthesia" is a word coined by French psychiatrist Benoit. To quote from his book, "the word 'coenaesthesis' indicates the total inner perception that we have of our organism. Besides the five senses by means of which we perceive the outside world, our coenaesthesis is a kind of sixth sense by means of which our organism perceives itself in its ensemble . . . coenaesthesis is a perception obtained by a decontraction."

II. TECHNIQUE:
TOWARD THE "NORMATIVE"

The body's movement is the most intimate essence
of our being alive. It is the basic material of dance. The
dance can be "good" only when the body, as it moves,
totally obeys nature. It moves as a river from its source,
as a spring in the Rockies until it flows into the ocean.
When gravity makes it fall in a boisterous rush, it does;
when the need of the land is level, it barely flows.[16]

The Normative Ideal

In 1951, Erick Hawkins founded both his own company and school
in New York City. In his attempt to develop a system of training that
would fulfill his desired aesthetic goals, Hawkins looked to science for an
affirmation of basic movement principles. In 1978, after twenty-seven
years of exploring and teaching his theories, Hawkins wrote the following
statement entitled, "On the Hawkins Technique." It is a brief introduction for the dance student to the importance of studying the scientific
truth behind movement training:

[16] Hawkins, *The Body Is a Clear Place*, p. 94.

An individual's name attached to a technique is a misnomer, in my opinion. By definition, Hawkins technique implies incompleteness, limitation, eccentricity.

It is true as in the wise Hindu saying, "before egotism, everything that is known is known in the mode of the knower."

But there is only one thing to be known if one is searching for the bedrock of knowledge, that is, what can be known by all knowers and therefore has some universal validity.

The first requirement of a correct dance training is, therefore, to train the novice only in the brightest, ascertainable, correct laws of moving according to scientific principles, that is according to nature. On this first level of the dance art, there can, as you see, be little room for personal interpretation.

Therefore, in my teaching, on the first level, my goal is to teach a novice only what is scientifically true and can be proven. I am working toward a GENERAL THEORY OF MODERN DANCE. The laws would be as true for a Hottentot, a New Yorker, or a citizen of Peking. . . .

Therefore, the basis of technique must be correctness according to nature, truth. The specialization of the principle of movement is what will make a great variety — not idiosyncrasy — of artists creating a rich culture.

More than ever in history, society needs the rich variety of powerful artists who don't ape science but who explore sensitivity and don't wipe out the senses.

Such are bald statements of the aesthetic aims I have for my School.[17]

---

[17] Erick Hawkins, School Brochure, July 25, 1978.

In his teaching, Hawkins referred to this "*General Theory of Modern Dance*" as "normative" or "generic" dance training. A "normative" ideal implies a common truth that is knowable and verifiable by all knowers. It is not *ab*normal, out of normalcy, but rather it is *in* harmony with itself and with its environment. Normative or generic dance training can, therefore, be defined as training that is in harmony with its own body and with the environment around it.

What Is Technique, What Is Style?

Hawkins often explained that it is important to understand the obvious yet often forgotten distinction between training dancers in dance *technique* and training dancers in particular movement *vocabularies* and *styles*. Because normative theories of movement are based on scientific fact, they have nothing to do with defining or comparing dance styles. Normative theories aim to discover and promote movement efficiency. Verifiable information about what constitutes efficient movement lies in the realm of movement science and *technique*. The shape and aesthetic choices governing the look of this movement have to do with movement *vocabulary* and *style*. If one were to analyze "good" Spanish, Indian, ballet, modern, tap, jazz or any other type of dancers, one would find that these dancers apply similar principles of kinetic efficiency.[18] Hawkins correctly knew that these two dance elements, technique and style, do not have to work at cross purposes:

> One danger is to confuse technique and vocabulary.
> For example, a person can have a very good vocabulary
> but have errors in technique, and, likewise, a person can
> have good technique and turn out a very dull dance.

---

[18] A strong trend toward applying this kind of "normative" theory in dance training can be seen in the increased application of universal principles found in "floor barre," Alexander technique, Pilates, Yoga, Trager, cranial/sacral, physical therapy, holistic awareness and other body/mind techniques in all dance training, regardless of style.

To find a complete art of dance we need the technique
and the vocabulary.[19]

Technique has the efficient fulfillment of scientific truth as its goal;
movement vocabulary and style aims to fulfill an aesthetic vision. Hawkins believed that in its purest form, normative movement training
is devoid of the idiosyncratic patterns and distortions from which any
dance style can be developed.

About Ideokinesis and Movement Imagery

Hawkins went about developing a system of normative dance training by entering into a lifelong study of kinesiology (the science of movement) and its offshoot science, ideokinesis (the study of the "idea" of
movement). Hawkins first studied ideokinesis briefly with its originator,
Mabel Todd, and later with two of Todd's disciples, Lulu Sweigard and
Barbara Clark.[20] The science of ideokinesis involves the study of the relationship between the mind, which governs "ideas" of movement, and the
body's movement response to those ideas. The main goal of analyzing
thought patterns during movement is to promote movement efficiency by
emphasizing correct neuromuscular-skeletal coordinations and postural
alignment. Improving movement efficiency through ideokinesis involves
1) becoming reacquainted with the structural facts of the human body
and 2) using movement imagery to change habitual neuromuscular-
skeletal patterns that impede maximum efficiency.[21]

---

[19] Hawkins, *The Body Is a Clear Place*, p. 138.

[20] The works of Mabel Todd and her followers Lulu Sweigard and Barbara Clark have provided the basis for the
majority of kinesiological application in the field of dance. Todd's writings include *Early Writings 1920–34*, *The
Thinking Body* (1937) and *The Hidden You* (1953). Sweigard's work, *Human Movement Potential* (1974), is yet
another excellent source of study for the dance student. This strain of ideokinesis continues to be taught in the
New York City area by Clark's pupil Andre Bernard and other ideokinesiologists, such as Dorothy Vislocky, Irene
Dowd, Karen Baracuda and Ann R. S. Poppen. Andre Bernard was first introduced to ideokinesis through Hawkins and later became Hawkins' primary link to the field. Bernard and Hawkins remained colleagues and friends
throughout Hawkins' lifetime.

[21] Neuromuscular-skeletal patterns are a three-part movement process. There is a 1) transfer of signals from the

Movement imagery can be applied in many ways, either during moments of stillness or when the body is in motion. When applied during moments of stillness, imagery is used to encourage change in what is called "involuntary" movement patterns, such as during normal respiratory activity or unconscious muscular contraction. "Voluntary" movement is movement that involves a conscious dialogue between the mind and the body when the body is in motion, such as in walking, running and dancing.

The goal of using imagery in involuntary movement is to increase one's sensitivity to optimal muscular coordination. Although muscles do not activate without nervous excitation, the central nervous system can fall into a pattern of engaging certain muscles during habitual movement patterns, whether or not these muscles are truly needed. It is as if to lift a leg the message from the brain is translated from "lift leg" to "engage all leg muscles." As a result, the muscles of the leg get into the habit of prematurely tensing and overworking. The primary movement goal becomes secondary to the activity of muscular contraction. By using movement imagery in moments of stillness, the dancer can correct these overworked neuromuscular-skeletal patterns.

"Thinking" a movement or imaging change within the body, gives the body the opportunity to return to innate, more efficient movement patterns. One imagery technique used by many movement trainers is to have students close their eyes and rethink a movement pattern as if they were watching themselves do it. Hawkins explained his own experience with this technique outside of dance:

> A few years ago I was in a position where I could
> have some diving lessons. As I watched the swimming

---

brain to the nervous system, 2) these signals elicit muscular contraction of the appropriate muscles to 3) activate the desired skeletal movement.

instructor teach some young boys, I was aware that they
always did the movement in the mind [first]. This correct placement of the muscle action through imagery
eliminates extra tension and its wrong placement on the
scale of contraction-decontraction. What the diving student learns by the process of doing it in the mind is
ease.[22]

By momentarily disengaging the body from *doing* the movement,
there is the potential to visualize an ideal form of the movement, devoid
of the mover's own idiosyncratic movement habits.

When adverse neuromuscular habits are successfully altered by using
movement imagery in moments of stillness, movement deficiency caused
by aberrant muscular patterns can be effectively corrected. However, it is
important to note that this type of subtle change is difficult to accom-
plish and requires extreme sensitivity and concentration. Minuscule
changes or sensations in a given area of the body can be sensed in a number of ways. Both the person experiencing change and (if applicable) the
person administering what is called "tactile aid"[23] will often feel the muscles twinge as habitually contracted muscles attempt to release; or a more
distinctive pulse or temperature change, signifying that more blood is
flowing through the area; or other indications from the activated part of
the body, signaling that internal adjustment is occurring. An example of
this type of change is often reflected most crucially in postural alignment
and in the lessening of surface tension in the muscles of the chest, back,
arms and legs.

[22] Hawkins, *The Body Is a Clear Place*, p. 133.
[23] *Tactile aid* is a term that describes the use of light touch to emphasize a location and line of direction for movement imagery in ideokinesis work.

Think/Feel

In Hawkins training, movement imagery is extensively used in both involuntary and voluntary movement work. Hawkins was particularly interested in the constant dialogue between the mind and body, which he termed the "think/feel" process. In describing his understanding of "think/feeling," he wrote:

> Whenever we see movement of a living creature, we know its movement through what is called the "kinesthetic sense."[24] The kinesthetic sense, the sensing of movement, is the heart of dance. . . .
>
> The main knowledge that comes out of the study of kinesiology is [therefore] life-giving and integrates the mind and the body with the precept "When you make an action, just do the movement." . . . When one understands the scientific reasoning behind kinesiology, one arrives at such unity of the body and mind that one simply "does the movement." It is a process of direct introspection of how the body feels in muscles and bones and in its overall esthesia—its common, undifferentiated feeling, sensation and tension.
>
> I run into student after student . . . who has been taught wrongly how to think/feel in the body. . . . When you make an action, just do the movement. No willfulness from the mind interferes with the movement by tightening the muscles erroneously. Tight muscles don't feel! Bound flow is trying to drive the car with the brakes on.[25]

---

[24] Hawkins, *The Body Is a Clear Place*, p. 124. Hawkins based his understanding of kinesis on the ancient Greek meaning of the word. The word "kine" is a Greek root meaning movement. The "cinema" is moving things, *movies*. "Aesthetic" is a Greek root meaning feeling. Anesthetic means not feeling. Kinesthetic means feeling of movement.
[25] Ibid., pp. 124, 128, 133.

Hawkins' reminder to just "do the movement" was a constant in his training. The implications of this simple directive are tremendous, echoing the philosophy that less is more. Inefficient postural alignment leads to overwork in the surrounding muscles. If the overworked muscles let go, the bones are left to find another, more efficient placement. For example, in attempting to decrease a lordosis, an exaggerated tilt of the pelvis forward (a postural pattern involving excessive contraction of the lower back muscles), the student, while either lying on the floor, sitting or standing, is encouraged to envision a wrapping forward from the center of the lower back toward the front of the pelvis. Instead of forcing the pelvis into a new posture, which often results in a reverse problem of *tucking* the pelvis, change is encouraged by releasing unnecessary muscular tension in the back (see Figure 1). One of the images used by Todd and Sweigard regarding this particular postural problem includes envisioning the back pockets of a pair of pants sliding sideways and to the front of the pants.[26]

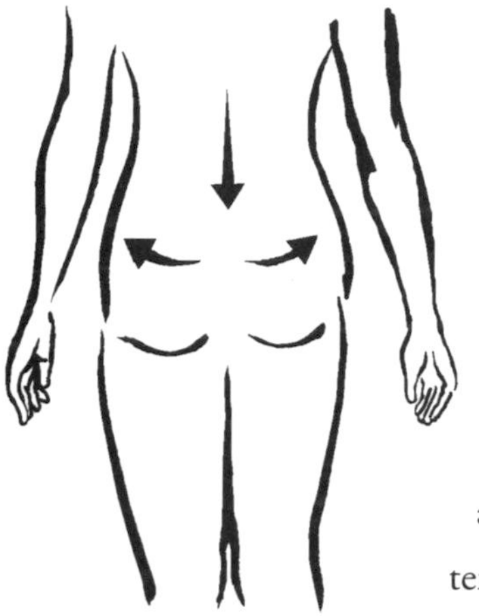

FIGURE 1. Releasing the Back Muscles

Similarly, to decrease tension of the rib cage manifested in the exaggerated lift of the chest, the image of Todd's closing umbrella is useful. By visualizing the ribs softening around the spine, as does the dome of an umbrella around its center pole, the ribs are encouraged to adjust back to a more restful position without having to force them into an unnaturally pushed down or held position.[27]

Some of the movement images coined by Hawkins as he developed his teaching are those of a "teeterbabe" support of the pelvis, the

---

[26] Mabel Todd, *The Thinking Body*, Paul B. Hoeber, Inc., New York, 1937, pp. 211–13.

[27] Ibid., pp. 211–13. For a further description of the umbrella image closing around the center pole of the spine, see Lulu Sweigard's *Human Movement Potential*, pp. 248–49.

"boomerang" swing of the legs, the "tasseling" flow of the arms and legs, and the ascending and descending curve of a "spiral staircase" through the axis of the leg. All of these images are designed to promote easy and efficient movement flow.

The distinction between involuntary and voluntary movement imagery is a delicate delineation to incorporate into a dance class. Both Sweigard and Todd were adamant about the importance of not participating in voluntary movement while using ideokinetic images so as not to replace one bad habit with another. Therefore, using metaphoric images or imaginative ways of describing a specific movement are invaluable teaching devices but require a great deal of sensitivity from both the teacher and student.

Who Is the Teacher?

Hawkins felt that the constant renewal of movement imagery prevents images from becoming stale and, therefore, ineffectual. A good teacher continually develops and renews his or her own favorite images. In this sense, keeping movement images fresh and alive is perhaps one of the most crucial functions of an effective teacher.[28]

Hawkins believed that a teacher does not actually "teach" a student. Rather, a teacher merely assists students in uncovering movement principles for themselves. The information a teacher is able to share with a student exists in the realm of fact and is, therefore, accessible to all who would seek it out. Hawkins frequently quoted from the writings of French Zen psychiatrist Hubert Benoit. In *The Supreme Doctrine*, Benoit summarized his concept of scientific fact and universal truth:

---

[28] An excellent resource for additional ideas on imagery can be found in Irene Dowd's beautiful work *Taking Root to Fly*, and Eric Franklin's two books, *Dynamic Alignment Through Imagery* and *Dance Imagery for Technique and Performance*.

> That which is valid, worthy of consideration, in the
> truth that I express does not belong to me-as-a-distinct-
> individual, and has not properly speaking any connexion
> with my particular person . . . the truth is not mine, or
> the property of any other man in particular; it is univer-
> sal. A claim to the paternity of any idea is absurd. . . .[29]

Hawkins paraphrased this idea: "If I speak a truth, it is not mine. If it is mine, it is not a truth." In this sense, Hawkins firmly believed that dance training based on movement truth is universally accessible and, therefore, devoid of any claim to authorship. It was Hawkins' hope that by coupling scientifically verifiable movement fact with an extensive use of movement imagery and sensitive movement experience, the "Hawkins" approach to training would allow the dancer to arrive at a core under-standing (both intellectually and physically) of how the body works and how it can work even more correctly, meaning more efficiently. Ultimately, the dancer is his or her own best teacher.

> So, the Hawkins technique, I really am embarrassed
> to use it . . . it's so partial and so egotistical. . . . What
> I'm after is a general theory of correct movement for our
> times. And so, it will not have anything to do with me.
> I will simply only be the vehicle for putting those true
> ideas into consciousness.
> If you know the scientific knowledge of the human
> body, whether you live in Asia, America, Africa, or wher-
> ever, you will not make mistakes in your movement that
> cause injury or limitation. Look, learn to discriminate,
> refine your perceptions.[30]

---

[29] Benoit, *The Supreme Doctrine*, p. 244.
[30] Hawkins, *The Body Is a Clear Place*, p. 122, and Erick Hawkins, Gail Myers interview.

III. PRINCIPLES

As stated previously, the idea of uncovering movement principles or "truths" is of primary importance to the Hawkins teaching philosophy. The principles presented here are only a beginning. Basing dance training on the physical capabilities and laws governing the human body offers endless possibilities. Each investigation of a different joint, muscle, neuromuscular pattern or physical principle can lead to further movement refinement and countless movement combinations. These refinements and combinations are left to the dancer's and choreographer's personal predilection. The following is only a brief look into basic movement principles incorporated by Hawkins into his dance training.

THE BODY'S CENTER OF GRAVITY: THE PELVIS

One of the fundamental principles Hawkins emphasized in his teaching was the importance of initiating and controlling movement from the body's center of gravity, located in the pelvis. He explained the sensation of moving from the center of gravity in the following way:

> The pearl of great price is the sensation of the center of gravity in the body, . . . the center where the largest, strongest, truly integrating muscles lie — in the front of the body, in the low belly, just where you can place your own right palm horizontally with the edge of the little finger lightly resting above the bone of the pubic symphysis.
>
> How to find words that indicate this experience to you is just about the hardest thing to do in all of dance teaching. I grope for words like "correct placement of the center." It is a direct introspection of the center of the organism, whereby awareness of all other parts of the body fall into harmonious co-ordering, which at the end we term "grace."[31]

The center of gravity in an object is that point around which the mass of that object rotates. It is the imaginary point by which an object can be perfectly balanced in relation to gravity and not experience any torquing or pulling away from balance. In the standing human body, this point is located roughly in front of the second sacral vertebra of the spine (see Figure 2). Its location varies slightly within each person according to body proportion. However, in a normal standing position, it is always located within the region of the pelvic girdle.

When the body assumes different positions during movement, the body's center of gravity also shifts. For example, a dancer's lifted arms raises the center of gravity. In this respect, there are times when a person's center of gravity is, technically speaking, outside of his or her body, as in a diver's pike position (see Figure 3). But, for most purposes, focusing on a sense of one's center of gravity in the pelvis serves as a useful point of departure for movement analysis and movement initiation. For the

---

[31] Hawkins, *The Body Is a Clear Place*, pp. 97–98.

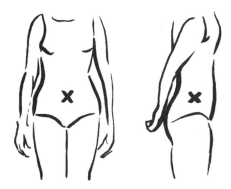

FIGURE 2. The Body's Center of Gravity

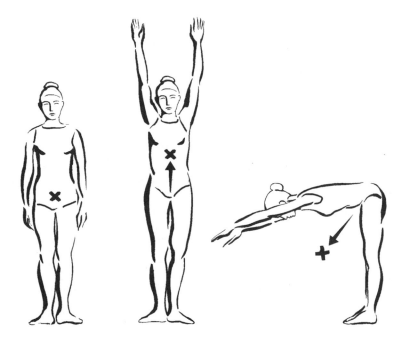

FIGURE 3. The Changing Location of the Body's Center of Gravity

dancer, becoming acquainted with this center of gravity of the body offers a clear point from which to move. The pelvis is the control center from which the other parts of the body extend.

As is well known in the science of physics, movement direction and velocity is determined by the direction and amount of an applied force. For example, in order to hit a billiard ball in a straight line, one must aim for the center of the cue ball; for the cue ball to travel at an angle, the player must aim at an "off-center" point on the cue ball even though the mass of the ball still revolves around its center (see Figure 4). This principle can also be applied in initiating movement of the human body. By initiating movement from the body's center of gravity in the pelvis, the dancer increases movement integration, which increases the potential force that can be directed toward a specific movement goal.

In addition to housing the body's center of gravity, the pelvis acts as a crucial foundation for the weight transfer of the upper body into the lower extremities. Designed to fulfill this weight-bearing function, the irregular, bowl-like shape of the pelvis is comprised of three pairs of fused bones, the iliac, the ischial and the pubic bones (see Figure 5).

In a standing or sitting position, weight travels through the spine into the legs, via the pelvis, passing along two sets of arched structures in the pelvis (see Figure 6). The first set of arcs involves a weight transfer through the sacral table (where lumbar and sacrum meet), along the "overcurve" of the sacroiliac crest. This weight then travels along the "undercurving" arcs of the ischial pubic arch, into the acetabular socket, where it is transferred into the femoral bones of the legs. The curved configuration of the two pairs of pelvic arches are perfectly designed for their weight transferring function, enabling a smooth, efficient transfer of weight similar to the way in which the sides of a cathedral wall are supported by the overcurving structures of a flying buttress, or the woven support of the undercurve of a basket or hammock.

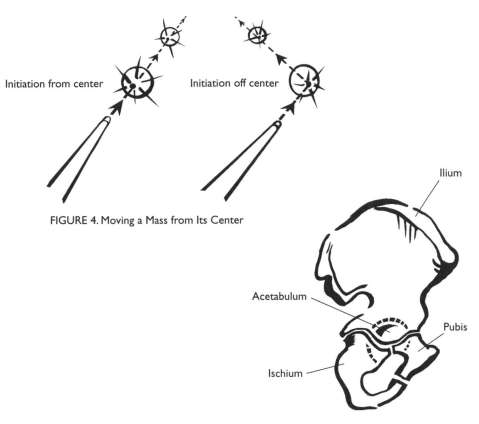

Initiation from center   Initiation off center

FIGURE 4. Moving a Mass from Its Center

Ilium

Acetabulum

Pubis

Ischium

FIGURE 5. The Bones of the Pelvis

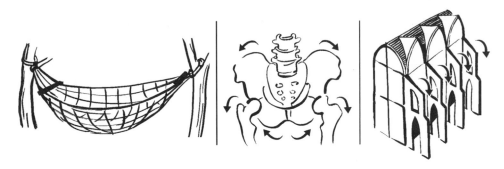

FIGURE 6. Pelvic Arches

Because the pelvis plays a crucial role in movement initiation and weight transfer, constant emphasis is placed on getting acquainted with its structure and potential power in movement. Much of the focus of a Hawkins class emphasizes reawakening the coenesthetic sense of initiating movement from the pelvis. Throughout a Hawkins class, students are encouraged to attempt initiation from this center, allowing the other parts of the body to engage only as a response to its initial force. This emphasis upon initiating movement from the body's center of gravity is a significant difference between the Hawkins method of training and other dance training. "Excentering" for Hawkins was:

> a violation of nature. When you have center, every-thing else goes along for the ride! You don't have to hold yourself. It's just your interest in combining your pelvis with your spine to find or sense the marvelous momen-tum through the skeleton.[32]

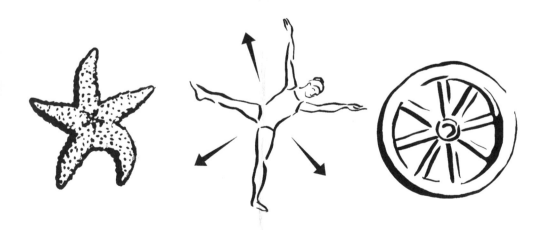

FIGURE 7. Images of Extending from the Center of Gravity

[32] Ibid.

Guiding movement from one's center of
gravity refocuses attention from the articulation of
the legs and arms to the body's movement from center.
The torso evokes the movement quality from which it radi-
ates the extremities. Frequent images for this sense of
central control include the image of a starfish (the
five points being two arms, two legs and the head)
or the image of the spokes of a wheel extending
from their central hub (see Figure 7).

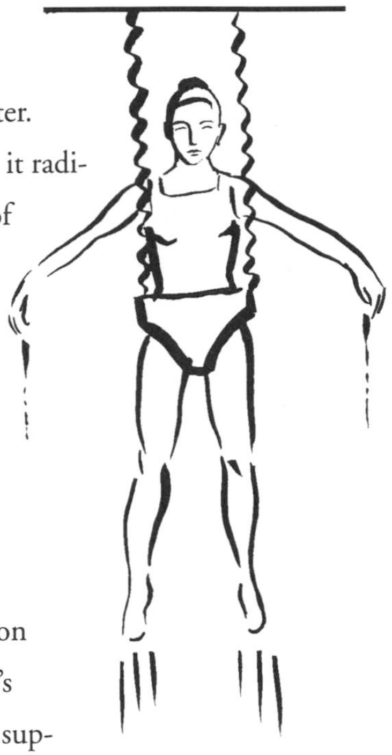

"Teeterbabe"

Perhaps the strongest image Hawkins used to
enhance a dancer's awareness of support and initiation
from the pelvis is that of being supported by a child's
"teeterbabe." A teeterbabe is a structure designed to support a baby's pelvis while allowing the baby's legs to
hang freely in the air (see Figure 8). As the baby's
pelvis, spine and upper body are supported by the

FIGURE 8.
The Lifted Support of the
"Teeterbabe"

seat, the legs have the freedom to dangle and swing. The beauty of this
image for dancers is that it allows the pelvis to have volume and weight,
much like a buoy uses its weight and volume to float on the water's surface. "Lifting" or "moving from center," in this sense, is not an ex-center-
ing of the upper body away from the pelvis, nor is it a holding or
gripping of the stomach and lower back muscles.

Using the teeterbabe image de-emphasizes the role of the legs as the
main basis of support for the body and enhances a clear sensation of balancing the pelvis and spine on top of the legs. It is a think/feel sensation
that can dramatically affect the placement of the entire body. Rather than
allowing weight to sit in the ball-and-socket joint of the hip, students are
encouraged to use the teeterbabe image of buoyancy and lift in the pelvis.

Feeling the legs dangling like a wasp's legs or imagining that the pelvis can float on top of the legs like a buoy on the water are some of the images that use this idea of integrated and buoyant pelvic control.

Quick weight shifts and suspensions over the tops of the legs are an ideal format for concentrating on the teeterbabe image. As the pelvis and spine glide across the floor, everything else can go along for the ride. The legs, arms and head can respond sensuously and freely.

The "Thigh" Sockets

Connected closely to moving from the body's center of gravity is the awareness of the body's largest and most powerful joints, the "thigh" sockets. Hawkins called the iliofemoral joints, or hip sockets, the thigh sockets because he felt that it was useful to focus attention on their function as the connecting joints between the pelvis and legs. Hawkins also found that imagining the thighs swinging from a narrow base under the pelvis, like a greyhound, was more integrating for movement than emphasizing the hips as a wide base of support, such as in the image of a mother carrying her baby

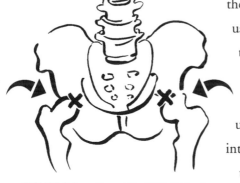

FIGURE 9. Location of the "Thigh" Sockets

on her "hips."[33] One of the most fascinatingly efficient aspects of the body's design is the placement of these two ball-and-socket joints in the pelvis (see Figure 9). They are not only the largest and heaviest joints in the body; they are also the closest mobile joints to the body's center of gravity, they have a tremendous amount of movement range and they have the important task of transferring weight from the pelvis and upper body into the legs. Understanding how to use these joints correctly is an often overlooked but important aspect of any dance training.

---

[33] The Hawkins term "thigh" socket is used throughout the text to refer to the iliofemoral joint. Todd refers to it as the "thigh joint."

A basic Hawkins movement designed to reawaken proper muscular coordination in the thigh socket is a simple "thigh socket flexion" done lying on the back during the floor warm up. While the front surface of the body rests toward the back of the spine, the leg is liberated from its common weight-bearing function and has the opportunity to experience a free range of motion. During a 1985 company class, Hawkins explained the thigh socket flexion:

> Now let's do a movement that is really almost the most profound movement experience there is for the human body in terms of moving bones, and that is to move at the thigh sockets. This sense about how you think/feel in the body is not common knowledge. I was studying for 16 years before my great teachers ever mentioned the thigh socket to me. And yet, if I really wanted to get down to the bedrock of movement experience . . . it would be to go right into the thigh socket.
>
> Take that first little thigh socket flexion, whereby one can isolate, not to the point that it is separate, but by trying, you might say, to organize the movement that goes into the rest of the leg and spine. Just flexing the thigh socket and letting the leg decontract. Letting the spine soften and not brace. Right in here, . . . the thigh flexion leads to the contraction of the front of the body, the biggest muscles that there are.
>
> This is not to make an overt sensation, but you almost want to say that this is pre-dancing. It's for the dancer, or for that matter anybody in regular life, to really understand where the key sensation of moving according to nature is done. It's right in that thigh socket. So, it's purely feeling. It's not theatrical in the sense that it's not showing movement. It's just that you are experiencing the movement.

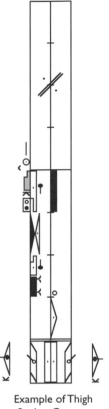

Example of Thigh Socket Creases

The biggest muscle in the body is the psoas — it connects the leg, the pelvis and the spine. Concomitantly, one has to think long down the muscles of the back so that you don't push the small of the back to the floor, but you permit it to go down to the floor because it's not being held against the flexing.[34]

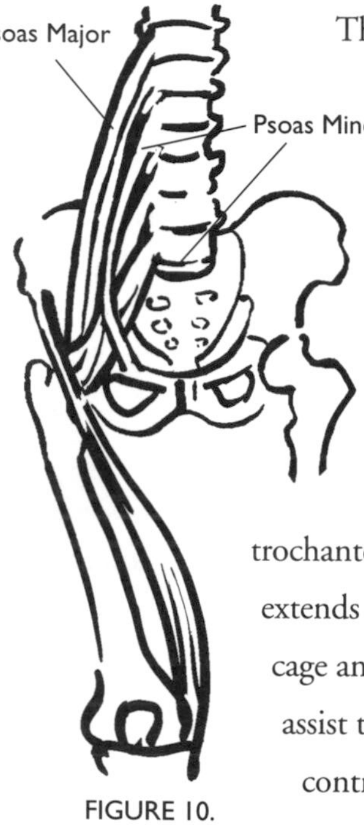

Psoas Major

Psoas Minor

FIGURE 10.
The Iliopsoas Muscles

The deeply located psoas (iliopsoas) muscles mentioned by Hawkins in this quote are key factors in any leg flexion. In fact, assisted only by a group of smaller muscles along the inner leg, they are the principal flexors of the thigh socket. The iliopsoas minor arises from the anterior side of the lower lumbar at L4 and L5, and inserts at the lesser trochanter of the femur bone. The iliopsoas major arises from the anterior side of the twelfth thoracic vertebra, also inserting at the lesser trochanter (see Figure 10). Remembering that the psoas major extends all the way up to the twelfth thoracic vertebra in the rib-cage and that both muscles are the major flexors of the thighs can assist the dancer in releasing excess quadricep and lower back contraction, thereby lengthening the entire front of the legs.

Shifting Weight

The challenge for dancers in finding stable balance during movement is to allow gravity to dictate the degree to which weight shift is necessary.[35] When shifting onto one leg in a vertical position, the plumb line of the body's weight toward gravity literally shifts from a pathway that travels close to the midline of the spine while on two legs, to somewhere along the weight-bearing side's shoulder and thigh socket joints (see

[34] For a complete illustration of this movement, see *The Erick Hawkins Modern Dance Technique Video*, Part I.
[35] For a further explanation of gravity and balance, see "Gravity, Weight, Balance and Alignment" in this chapter.

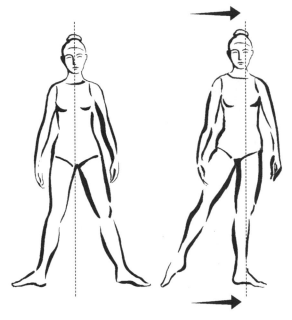

FIGURE 11.
Shifting the Vertical Axis

Figure 11). Therefore, being acquainted with the amount and location of weight shift necessary for controlled movement is a fundamental skill for the dancer to master. Hawkins consistently stressed the importance of being able to quickly shift and catch weight in a deep thigh socket "crease." Many movement patterns during center floor focus on cultivating this quick weight shift onto the top of the leg. A frequent standing movement for this purpose involves shifting weight onto one leg while the other leg extends behind the body in an "arabesque" position. Once the weight is shifted securely onto the standing leg, the leg can then soften into the thigh socket, knee and ankle joints (see Figure 12). Being able to gather one's weight into a deep thigh socket crease offers more control than would a similar balance executed by relying on muscular contraction for stability.

FIGURE 12.
A Standing Thigh Socket Crease

"Undercurves" and "Overcurves"

Directly related to the ideas of teeterbabe support of the pelvis and the importance of shifting one's weight from a fully integrated center of gravity is the principle of the under- and overcurve pathways of the pelvis. Due to the body's structural design, the path described by efficient movement flow travels along curves and arcs (see in this chapter, "Arcs, Curves and Momentum"). As Hawkins explained it:

> The U-shape is just one of the two paths that all movement has to follow. . . . You're always going to have some sort of a curve — under or over. There are only two ways to throw an apple, or a baseball . . . or to enter a jump . . . [it describes] some kind of an arc [an over curve or an under curve].[36]

There are no straight bones in the human body. This is a beautifully strong and resilient way in which the body is designed to absorb weight

---

[36] Erick Hawkins, *The Erick Hawkins Modern Dance Technique Video*, Part I.

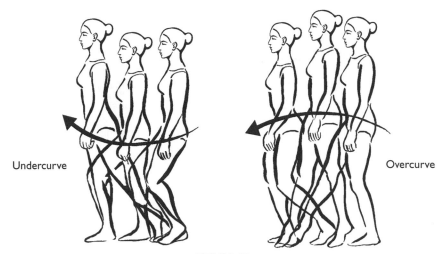

Undercurve   Overcurve

FIGURE 13.
Under- and Overcurved Pathways of the Pelvis

and move efficiently. The structure of the legs and pelvis determines the arced path that the pelvis follows during weight shifts. If, from a standing position, the leg joints lengthen or begin from a creased position and then travel through a lengthened position during a weight shift, the path of the pelvis will outline an overcurved path. If these same leg joints crease during a weight shift, the pelvis will move in an undercurved path (see Figure 13).

The terms "undercurve" and "overcurve" are constantly used in a Hawkins technique class as a way in which to define the pathway of movement of the pelvis. Attuning the student to the directions of these overcurving and undercurving weight shifts achieves two goals: It focuses the student's attention on redirecting the initiation of movement from the pelvis, and it introduces the student to the concepts of curved flow traveling through the entire body. When the pelvis successfully lifts and clearly articulates through these curved pathways, the dancer can achieve, with minimal strain, a precise way of working on top of the thigh sockets, which results in a buoyant and floating quality of movement.

GRAVITY, WEIGHT, BALANCE AND ALIGNMENT

Two of the fundamental principles affecting all human movement are gravity and a body's optimal alignment in relationship to gravity. All mass is pulled toward the earth by gravity and is met with an equal force thrusting in opposition upward to support that mass. In the standing or sitting human body, gravity and its oppositional force is experienced through a sense of weight and the challenge of balancing that weight.

The Spine and Spinal Alignment

The skeletal structure of the human body is designed to cooperate with gravity in order to maintain balance and execute movement. The spine, as the main weight-bearing structure of the axial skeleton (torso, neck and head) is designed to transfer weight through a system of four spinal curves (see Figure 14). The sacral curve of the pelvis and thoracic curve of the rib cage exist from birth. The cervical curve of the neck develops as a baby begins to raise his or her head against gravity. The lumbar curve, between the pelvis and rib cage, develops as the baby begins to crawl and walk. These four curves develop to counterbalance each other as a way of absorbing the constant impact of weight transfer.

The line of gravity that passes through the curves of the spine forms a vertical axis.[37] Think of a direct plumb line of weight traveling down through the center of this vertical axis, transferring into the pelvis through the sacral table (where the lumbar meets the sacrum) and into the legs through the heads of both femur bones (see Figure 15). By using

---

[37] Hawkins would often refer to the "linea alba" within the body as a visual reference point for the vertical axis. The linea alba is, literally, a "white line" of tendon that runs vertically along the center of the abdomen, from the sternum to the pubic symphysis. Although it is not the actual vertical axis of the body's weight, the term is used in Hawkins classes to refer to a center-line marker along which to orient the hands. For example, Hawkins would encourage dancers to let a hand gesture pass down along the linea alba.

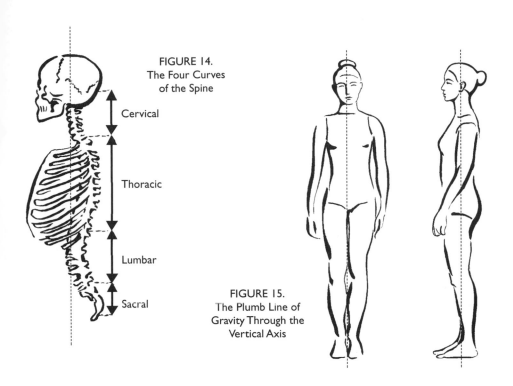

FIGURE 14.
The Four Curves
of the Spine

Cervical

Thoracic

Lumbar

Sacral

FIGURE 15.
The Plumb Line of
Gravity Through the
Vertical Axis

the images of weight transferring down the spine into the earth and a sense of the counteractive energy traveling up the spine from the earth, the dancer can maintain a powerful connection to the center of his or her weight while dynamically lengthening through the body. It is important to note that this sense of counterstretch is possible only when the body is properly aligned both vertically and sagittally.[38] Therefore, the search for capturing the sensation of true center begins in reawakening a sense of proper alignment.

Former Hawkins company member Beverly Brown beautifully expresses this image of finding a dynamically centered verticality:

[38] The terms "vertical," denoting side-to-side planes, and "sagittal," denoting front to back planes, are commonly used dance terms derived from Hungarian movement theorist Rudolf Laban's extensive research in space harmony.

I learned from Erick that often the best way to clarify a movement idea is through the use of a metaphor. One of the most powerful yet simple images to express what it means to find your center is this: As a tree grows taller with wider-reaching branches, it will always grow a thicker trunk and deeper roots. The tree "knows" what to do for stability. Man's mind, on the other hand, can invent possibilities that are not necessarily good for his body. He may try to reach away from himself without, at the same time, growing deep roots. If we are to learn from nature, we must know where it is we are standing at the same time that we search for the north star.[39]

Think of a direct plumb line traveling through the center of your vertical axis. Cathy Ward in *Agathlon*, 1980.

In the process of "reaching away from oneself," the dancer can often fall into an inefficient alignment pattern. Deviation from an ideal alignment causes imbalances throughout the whole body as the body attempts to maintain its balance against the force of gravity.[40]

One of the primary functions of bone is to support weight. The primary function of muscle is to move bone. The body's natural impulse is to maintain balance. Therefore, if the vertebrae of the spine are manipulated or distorted in their relationship to one another (not allowing them to efficiently support weight), the muscles around the vertebrae unnecessarily engage in an attempt to help

[39] Beverly Brown, "Training to Dance with Erick Hawkins," *Erick Hawkins: Theory & Training*, ed. Richard Lorber, American Dance Guild, Inc., New York, 1979, p. 12.
[40] Todd, *The Thinking Body*, pp. 45–77.

the body find and maintain balance. The contraction of these muscles restricts range of motion, causing the body to work harder and with greater strain and risk of injury than it would if it were properly aligned.

Hawkins often explained this principle of proper alignment by using the simple example of children's building blocks resting one on top of the other. The three main weights of the spine are like three blocks: the pelvis block, the rib-cage block and the head block. If one of these blocks gets nudged over to one side, the whole tower of blocks can easily topple over. The same is true for the spine. For example, if someone carries a heavy object on his or her right side, the body

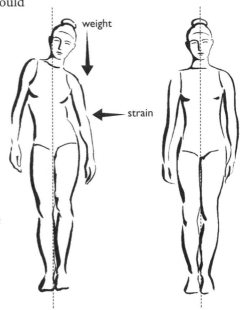

FIGURE 16.
Lateral Spinal Alignment

compensates for this weight by shifting the spine to the left, causing a change in the normal pattern of compression through the vertebrae as the body adjusts to an abnormal distribution of weight (see Figure 16). After carrying the object for a certain length of time, the carrier will experience some sort of discomfiture or pain in the back as the body is called upon to balance itself in a way that is alien to its natural structure.

One of the most basic ways in which Hawkins illustrated his constant awareness of the importance of correct body alignment occurred outside the dance studio. Regardless of his years around dancers and their enormous dance bags, Hawkins was continually amazed at the volume of "stuff" his dancers carried around, usually over one shoulder. Immediately he would ask the dancer to take the bag off of his or her shoulder, explaining how the load was adversely affecting the body's correct spinal alignment. The most efficient way of carrying a heavy load is to balance the weight equally between the right and left sides of the spine (as in the balanced weight of a knapsack resting on both shoulders).

Being familiar with these principles of gravity, spinal alignment and balanced weight is an invaluable tool for the dancer. Under ideal application in dance training, they contribute to a dancer's movement efficiency and flow. In the classroom, the awareness of body alignment is encouraged throughout class in various ways. The first step in returning to a useful postural alignment involves letting go of detrimental habits. Typical areas affected by bad posture are the lower back, chest, shoulders and neck.

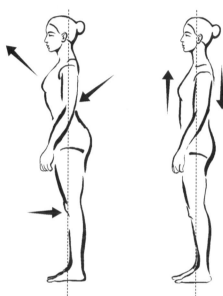

FIGURE 17.
Correcting Postural Habits in the Spine

Frequently dancers have the habit of overtensing the lumbar muscles, resulting in a visible lordosis of the spine (see Figure 17).[41] By encouraging the lumbar muscles to release and lengthen, the anterior/posterior tilt of the pelvis can be decreased. The decreased tilt eases strain on anterior pelvic ligaments, frees the range of motion around the thigh sockets and enhances a truer sense of spinal balance in relation to the joints. Balancing doing and not-doing is crucial when correcting these postural patterns. Actively trying to correct a pelvic tilt by "tucking" the pelvis under in the opposite direction is an equally effortful and inefficient postural habit. Ideal alignment aims toward releasing all unnecessary effort while maintaining balance.

---

[41] Lordosis of the spine also tends to put an additional strain on the back of the knees. The body counteracts weight collapsing forward in the spine by pulling weight back in the legs.

Another typical habit for dancers is to exaggerate the lift of the chest. Hawkins called this tendency "puffing out the chest" (see Figure 17). The danger in this habit is that the back of the rib-cage muscles stay in permanent contraction, affecting lung capacity and range of motion in the thoracic and cervical spine, and causing undue pressure on the kidneys. When intercostal, chest and shoulder girdle muscles are at ease, the weight of the rib-cage rests off an easily supported sternum, and cervical/thoracic spine. As a result of less tension in the chest, rib-cage and thoracic spine, movement range and respiratory capacity increases.

Yet another pattern is for dancers to take unnecessary tension in the shoulders so that they rise up toward the ears, putting further strain on the neck (see Figure 18). Therefore, connected

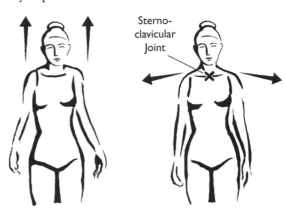

FIGURE 18.
Releasing Excess Shoulder Tension

with the idea of allowing the sternum to fall back toward center is the goal of letting the shoulder girdle be supported from the sternum. It is often useful to remember that the entire bony structure of the shoulder and arm originates from the sternoclavicular joint. The shoulder girdle and arms extending and resting from this point create a type of drapery around the egg shape of the ribs.[42] By visualizing this image and applying it to one's own body, the habit of holding the shoulders up diminishes and the shoulder structure's true weight can be more easily balanced and manipulated from the spine. Letting the shoulders extend outward from the sternoclavicular joint increases movement range in the shoulder

[42] Additional images for letting the shoulders and arms drape over the ribs are described in Todd, *The Thinking Body*, pp. 156–57.

joint, lessens tension in the neck and allows the arms to swing more freely from the top of the humerus (upper arm) bone.

Leg Alignment

The second most crucial area directly affected by gravity and weight balance is leg alignment. Here, too, the principle of efficient alignment in relationship to gravity applies. Alignment and mobility in the leg involves movement in three joints: the thigh socket, the knee and the ankle. All three joints organize around a common axis of the leg similar to the way in which all folds of a concertina or joints of a car jack work in unison (see Figure 19). If one were to isolate each joint (an activity virtually impossible to do in a standing position), the integrity of the vertical axis through these joints would be destroyed (see Figure 20). In most normal activity, all three joints act as a group around a common axis of the leg.

Regardless of whether or not the dancer stands in parallel or in a turned-out position, an ideal leg alignment, as continually stressed by physical therapists and movement specialists, involves keeping these three

FIGURE 19.
Integration and the "Hierarchy"
of Ideal Leg Alignment

FIGURE 20.
Nonintegration of the Leg Joints

Knees and Ankles Only   Thigh Sockets and Knees Only   Thigh Sockets and Ankles Only

joints of the leg (the thigh socket, the knee and the ankle) and the second and third toes along the same linear axis. Allowing the knee to either supinate (as in a bowlegged alignment) or pronate (as in a knock-kneed alignment) puts an incredible amount of strain on the cartilage, tendons and ligaments of the knee and ankle and is an inefficient alignment pattern. Unfortunately, knee and ankle injuries, largely due to poor leg alignment, are two of the most common among dancers. By taking the time to repattern leg coordination and alignment, the risk of these injuries can be greatly diminished.

"Hierarchy" of the Legs

Hawkins often spoke of proper leg coordination and alignment as being organized through a "hierarchy" of leg movement. Because of its proximal orientation in relation to the body's center of gravity and because of its structural power as the largest joint in the human body, the thigh socket is an ideal initiator of leg movement. All leg movement, even the simple dorsiflexion of the ankle, has some sort of muscular or bony dependence upon the intricate connection of muscles, tendons and ligaments that cross and/or originate from the area of the thigh socket.

Therefore, achieving efficiently integrated leg movement involves honoring this natural powerhouse.

Moving through the hierarchy of the leg means that the dancer is aware of sensation and initiation of leg movement from the thigh socket, close to the center of gravity, and not simply from an isolated knee or ankle action. In this way, keeping the image of a hierarchy of the leg assists in integrating leg movement from one's pelvic center. All three joints work in harmony toward achieving one clear, smooth movement.

These and other goals for correct spinal and leg alignment are frequently explored throughout a typical Hawkins approach to technique. Once again, the primary principle unifying all of these observations is the idea of allowing as much weight as possible to fall toward gravity along the vertical axis of the spine and legs. The body is in search of constant balance in relationship to the forces of gravity. One neither succumbs completely to gravity nor completely attempts to defy gravity. Only by cooperating with gravity can the body stay erect and move in its most naturally free-flowing form.[43]

Many other technical elements are emphasized during technique classes. However, continually returning to one's own sense of center and one's own vertical axis is an ever-present challenge for the dance student. Working in this way offers control over one's balance (dancers call this being "centered" or "on one's legs") without relying upon overwork or unnecessary stress to achieve this control.

CONTRACTION AND "DECONTRACTION"

Connected to the principles of gravity and efficient body alignment are the principles of muscular contraction and release, or "decontraction,"

---

[43] Modern dance pioneer Doris Humphrey centered her technique around investigations of gravity and balance, calling movement between falling to and rebounding from gravity the "arc between two deaths." Doris Humphrey, *The Art of Making Dances*, Grove Press Inc., New York, 1959, p. 106.

as Hawkins preferred to call it. Contraction and decontraction are principles that involve the balance of doing and not-doing in the muscles.
Hawkins carefully described this muscular activity:

> Every person, and therefore every dance student, is
> always in between the extreme states of contraction and
> decontraction of the muscles. Complete contraction of
> all the muscles in the body creates a catatonic state, and
> complete decontraction of all muscles is similar to
> fainting. . . .
>
> Every person needs to find the correct place on this
> scale of contraction/decontraction to do what is needed
> to be done. The brain tells one the movement that one
> wants to do. The image in the brain decides whether it's
> a movement of contraction or decontraction. . . .
>
> One might question how to find this correct place-
> ment on the scale of contraction and decontraction for
> any given movement. The answer is a kind of feeling
> introspection in the body that leads one into doing the
> correct effort for any movement. The kinesiological rule
> is to just do the movement. If the movement is a slash,
> you can't bind the movement or grip the muscles to
> make the slash. Or if the movement is to pat someone
> on the behind, you don't have to grip the muscles in
> order to do the movement. The tenderness in the mind
> takes care of the movement in the action. . . .
>
> For the body to work best, muscle must decontract,
> and therefore, at that moment, have lovelier move-
> ment.[44]

This constant introspection of finding the correct amount of effort
needed for each movement is a main focus of perfecting technique. The

---

[44] Hawkins, *The Body Is a Clear Place*, pp. 124–34.

goal is ease and efficiency so that the body can perform at its optimal energy level.

The contraction of a muscle initiates movement. The amount of movement power a muscular contraction generates is determined by the amount of contraction executed. In Hawkins training, the balance between contraction and decontraction is continually emphasized: One cannot effectively move the skeleton without the other. Signals from the nervous system cause muscular contraction and decontraction in order to move the skeleton. The natural state of the muscles tends toward decontraction until called upon to execute movement.[45] A *de*contracted muscle is a muscle that has *released* its tensile state. If the muscle is healthy and sensitive to neural commands, a contraction originating from this more naturally decontracted state has more potential power than a similar activity originating from an already tense muscle.[46]

The decontraction of muscle not only allows the body to find its most efficient spinal alignment and movement pathway, but also helps the muscle to maintain its elasticity and sensation. Hawkins continually argued that one cannot know if one is doing something harmful to the body if one cannot "feel" the body. Hawkins' steadfast reminder to stay alert to muscular sensation relates to his interest in refining coenesthetic sensation. As he observed throughout his years of dance training and teaching, the dancer often risks losing the ability to feel bodily sensation because of the overdevelopment of muscle. "Tight muscles don't feel," was a regular Hawkins admonition. Hawkins also argued that once this coenesthetic sense is deadened, the dancer loses the natural sensitivity toward his or her own *humanness*.[47] As he writes:

[45] In optimal alignment, only a few muscles need to be active. The counterbalance of various axes of rotation and respective ligamentous structures fulfill the remaining balancing tasks.

[46] Graham training, as Hawkins experienced it in the 1940s, emphasized muscular contraction to such an extreme that often the importance of *releasing* the muscles was completely neglected.

[47] For further reading regarding Hawkins' ideas on sensation and the human spirit, see his essays, "Modern Dance as a Voyage of Discovery," pp. 12–37, and "Dance as a Metaphor of Existence," pp. 99–119, in his *The Body Is a Clear Place*.

Sensuousness is effortless and has no sense of the dominating exhilaration of competitive achievement, nor of the morbid excitement of aggressive violence. Sensuousness is impossible with tight muscles. Tight muscles cannot feel. They turn the supple human body into a distorted and injured machine. Only effortless, free-flowing muscles are sensuous. . . .

Sensuous is living in the now, in immediacy; therefore, there is no alienation. Here the body is a clear place. Sheer living is immediately experienced through one's own physical being in the very tasting of the total feast of the world around.[48]

In support of this coenesthetic way of working, Hawkins often related two stories of serious injuries he had had during his ballet and Graham years. From his years of ballet training he had been in the habit of tensing and holding all of the muscles along the front of the chest. Because of this constant muscular contraction, the anterior rib and chest muscles lost their ability to soften and release. One day while dancing he overstretched these already overly contracted muscles and they tore away from his sternum. It took a year for his body to heal from this injury.[49]

Hawkins had a similar accident, involving the Achilles' tendon and calf muscle, when dancing with Graham. He had been overworking the muscles of the lower leg to such a degree that they became overly developed and, therefore, too muscle-bound to sense harmful movement habits. One day in rehearsal, having overtaxed the calf muscle and Achilles' tendon, Hawkins experienced a stretch reflex[50] in the leg, which resulted in a severe injury. In his words, the calf and Achilles' just "gave

---

[48] Hawkins, *The Body Is a Clear Place*, pp. 69–71.

[49] Hawkins often related this story of his chest injury when trying to explain the beauty of "yielding" and "softening" in the chest, as opposed to continually bracing and pushing forward in that area of the body.

[50] Stretch reflex occurs when a muscle reaches its maximal stretch: the nervous system signals a contraction in the muscle in an attempt to protect it from being injured. If this signal is ignored and the muscle is stretched beyond the reflexive limit, a serious strain or tear of the muscle can occur.

up." He realized then that it was not useful to rely on force to direct movement. If a muscle is constantly in "contracture" (a permanently contracted state), sensation in that muscle is lost, and the range of movement in the surrounding joints is inhibited, affecting kinetic flow and overall movement efficiency. A charley horse in the calf muscle is a typical result of this prolonged muscular contracture.

It is important to note that the decontraction of a muscle can be visualized in a number of ways. Some students often interpret the idea of decontraction as a passive collapse of the muscle. To some degree, the decontraction of muscle does imply a "yielding" to gravity. However, yielding does not mean collapsing! If water spills onto the floor, it immediately spreads out along the floor in all directions. It does not drop and stay exactly where it falls like an ice cube or a lead balloon. The image of a decontraction can be used as an active spreading or lengthening of muscle rather than a passive dropping of muscle weight. In this sense, a decontraction is *active*, not *passive*, and does not have a limp or collapsed quality.

Moving efficiently and gracefully requires the constant interplay between the actions of contraction and decontraction, similar to the seamless regularity of inhaling and exhaling without holding one's breath. In ideally experienced muscle patterns, there is both an awareness and a sensation of contraction and an equal sensation of the muscle actively lengthening out of this contracted state. Allowing the muscles to lengthen through a decontraction also conserves potential movement energy more efficiently than would a passive softening in the muscle because there is no stop in movement flow. The idea is to let go, lengthen and unbind energy into its infinite flow.

Often, students with extensive dance training cannot easily incorporate this distinction between a collapsed decontraction and a lengthened decontraction into their movement because they have an underdeveloped ability to even slightly decontract the muscles. Typically, these students

The balance of doing and not doing in the muscles. Gloria McLean in *Early Floating*, 1990.

must first challenge their muscles to experience complete release. Only after the muscles have regained this ability to soften and sense weight is an actively lengthened decontraction possible.

Hawkins often illustrated the danger of either giving in completely to a collapsed decontraction or attempting to defy gravity in muscular contraction by relating two stories. The first story involved the sensation of fainting. While giving blood at a doctor's office one day, all of his muscles went completely limp. As a result of a lack of muscular tension, Hawkins fell to the ground.

By contrast, Hawkins related a second story about being with a student when the student went into a catatonic state. As Hawkins described it, all of the dancer's muscles froze in contraction, losing their ability to balance the body against the pull of gravity. The student, similar to Hawkins in the doctor's office, also fell to the ground, but this time because of his inability to *release* the muscles. These two extreme responses to muscular contraction and the pull of gravity illustrate the importance of finding the appropriate relationship between gravity, balance and muscular sensation.

For Hawkins, muscular sensation is closely related to man's fundamental view of the body. Using the classical Greek ideal of human beauty as his model, Hawkins felt that correct movement of the body leads to beautiful movement, and beautiful movement forms a beautiful body. Hawkins explained his thoughts on the subject:

> The most primal birthright of the human organism is that it must move muscle. After all, our life is the movement of our heart muscle and everybody knows that the minute that heart muscles stops, we're dead—and there ain't nothing there! You can talk about the afterlife, and spirits, and about God up there, or heaven . . . but if you can just recognize that this earth is paradise, then you might bring *this* life to its full potential. . . .
>
> [A]nd so, what a peculiar idea is our general notion that there's something demeaning about nakedness. You look at the Greek vases and you can't imagine that anybody could exist without the body being brought to great sensitivity, fulfillment and beauty. The beauty of muscles comes from their correct proportion of action. If you use them too much, they're gross, if you don't use them enough, they're feeble. The criterion of beauty begins right from the movement of the body. . . .[51]

[51] Erick Hawkins, Gail Myers interview.

If one were to watch dancers with this idea of contraction and decontraction in mind, one would immediately notice the difference between dancers who overuse their muscles and those who do not. The general difference would be seen in their movement flow, connections and transitions. Dancers who utilize a wide range of contraction and decontraction will not only be more sensuously engaged in their movement and able to readily shift weight, but also will generally appear to be more uninhibited in their movement flow. By contrast, dancers who move with constantly contracted muscles will probably seem to have more brittle or abrupt movement flow. The use of muscular decontraction and awareness of muscular sensation are perhaps two of the most noticeable aspects of the Hawkins technique.

"Tassels"

A common Hawkins image that makes use of an active decontraction is the image of the limbs acting as tassels. If the muscles in the arms and legs are allowed to decontract sufficiently, they will respond organically to movement initiated from the torso. The movement pathways these loose limbs follow are similar to the natural momentum paths of the loose end

FIGURE 21. The Arms and Legs as Tassels

of a rope, or a tassel on the end of a hat or curtain, or the dangling sensation of a loose tooth (see Figure 21).

This quality of tasseling the limbs from a very active spine greatly enhances movement flow and dynamic range. For example, a Hawkins "tassel-leg turn" begins with the pelvis spiraling toward or away from a weight-bearing leg. As the pelvis continues to spiral over the ball of the standing foot, the nonweight-bearing leg unleashes in response to the impetus of the pelvis. If properly decontracted and integrated with the pelvis, the weight of this trailing leg will acquire enough momentum to continue "tasseling" around the pelvis and spine beyond the initial pelvic impetus (see Figure 22).

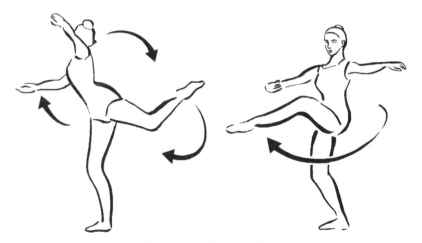

FIGURE 22. A Tassel-Leg Turn
(The leg swings around like the loose end of a rope)

When responding like tassels, legs and arms unwrap from the initiation of the pelvis and spine much like the unwrapping of a tether ball and rope from around a center pole. Tassel images evoke a quality of fluidity and ease that is very different from putting the arm or leg into one fixed position either to the front, side or back. It is not that one form is right or wrong. However, a tassel leg is governed by principles different from a

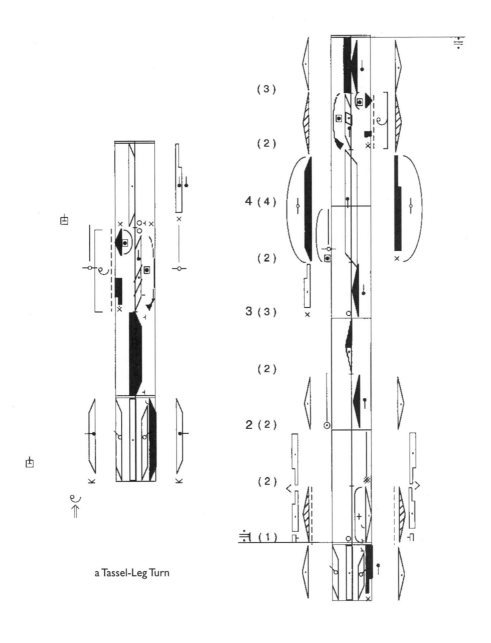

(3)

(2)

4 (4)

(2)

3 (3)

(2)

2 (2)

(2)

(1)

a Tassel-Leg Turn

a Tassel-Leg Turn Combination

"placed" leg. Hawkins repeatedly emphasized that no movement, if it obeys a natural principle, is wrong. The well-rounded choreographer, teacher and student strive to have mastery over a wide variety of ways in which to move, so that they do not fall victim to the limits of always doing something in the same way.

One of the useful things to remember about the tassel image is that its fullest manifestation is contingent on the quality of integration near its central initiation. In other words, the distal aspects of the limbs can truly let go and tassel only if the dancer is securely integrated from center. Otherwise, the weight of the loose leg will have the tendency to pull the dancer "off-center," which is, of course, a possibility for choreography and a useful sensation if the distinction between "centered" and "off-centered" movement is made clear. However, as a general training principle, "tasseling" most often assumes that the tasseling body part is controlled from center.

ARCS, CURVES AND MOMENTUM

The principle of momentum defines the force of motion acquired by a moving body as a result of the continuance of its motion. Coasting (e.g., traveling on a bicycle without having to peddle) is an example of momentum. So, too, is the accelerating force of a falling ball responding to the pull of gravity (see Figure 23). In both cases, movement continues beyond the initial application of force. The same is true in movement of the human body. If human movement is uninterrupted by overwork or an outside force, the body will continue to travel along the most efficient and effortless route possible.

Using momentum is one of the key factors in achieving the kind of effortless movement toward which Hawkins aimed. He observed that by taking advantage of the "continuance" of a body's movement, a dancer

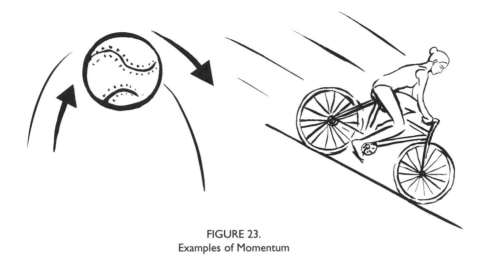

FIGURE 23.
Examples of Momentum

can allow movements their most efficient and organic execution. For example, force is required to fight gravity in lifting an arm overhead. Once the arm reaches the apex of the movement and begins its descent, new force is no longer needed during the descent because gravity creates sufficient momentum for the movement to occur. Hawkins often pointed out that dancers are so accustomed to the idea of "working" to achieve all of their movement that they very often lose the ability to sense and use the momentum already acting on their bodies.

Just as there are no straight lines in the body, there are no straight lines in human movement. All human movement describes arcs and curves. Therefore, momentum in the body also manifests itself in curved patterns. Joints act as the fulcrum for the bones. In the same way that the circumferential end of the radius of a circle describes an arc when rotated from center, the distal end of a bone travels in an arc around its fulcrum (see Figure 24). For example, when a dancer executes a straight-legged swing of the leg (either to the front, side or back), the distal end of the moving leg (i.e., the toes) will describe a curve in the air. In a two-dimensional plane these curved pathways can connect either 1) along an

55

S-shaped path or 2) along a circular or looping path (see Figure 25). When these curves are considered three-dimensionally, the number of curved pathways a movement can describe becomes vast.

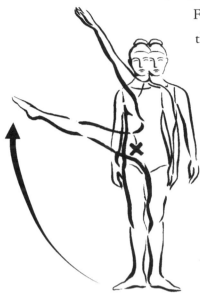

FIGURE 24. The Thigh Socket as the Center of an Arc

FIGURE 25. Curved Pathways of Movement Flow

FIGURE 26.
Momentum of a Figure 8

Loops and the "Figure 8"

Arcs that extend out and fall back toward center describe loops. The beauty of continuously looping energy in movement is that the body is constantly in a position to regenerate its energy. Therefore, a dancer who masters the ability to toss away from and return weight and momentum back to center will be continually renewing an impetus from center. A basic Hawkins image of the loop is the shape of a figure 8. The beauty of following a figure 8 as a pathway for movement flow is that it is comprised of a series of loops along which movement can travel virtually endlessly as a result of the potential momentum inherent within its structure (see Figure 26). It is the sign of infinity used in mathematics and physics: infinite movement potential. One of its most frequent uses within a Hawkins class is in describing the path of the arms (see "Quarter Turns" and "Figure 8s" in chapter IV).

"Boomerangs"

Another Hawkins image that involves the idea of looping movement and momentum is the "boomerang." The boomerang is yet another principle that uses momentum to spin away from and back to center (see Figure 27). Hawkins instructors frequently use the image of the legs moving as a boomerang to enhance smooth leg integration as legs "toss" away from and return to the acetabular fulcrum in the thigh socket (see "boomerangs" in chapter IV). Similar to the sensation in a tassel, a boomerang sensation in the limbs is contingent on a strong central control in the pelvis (or spine and shoulder girdle, in the case of an arm boomerang), and a true sensation of weight in

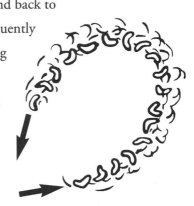

FIGURE 27.
Momentum of a Boomerang

the limbs to allow momentum to carry them through the action. The leg does not have to be "kicked" or put into any position, nor does the arm have to be "carried" or "held" if the sensation of boomeranging momentum is fully incorporated into the movement.

Spirals

Throughout Hawkins training, the image of the curved path of a spiral is frequently used to describe and enhance movement efficiency and flow. One of Hawkins' favorite movement ideas, the image of a descending or ascending spiral, promotes smooth rotation in the spine and easeful turn-out and weight shift through the legs. In the curved path of a spiral, the direct downward force of gravity is diverted through a gradually descending curve that wraps around a vertical axis. Using this spiral image prolongs and thereby softens the force of descending weight, while encouraging a lengthened vertical axis (see "Quarter Turns" and "Turns and the Spiral Staircase" in chapter IV).

As can be seen from the examples of the tassel, boomerang and spiral, utilizing the law of momentum as it acts upon the body can assist the dancer in liberating movement flow. By considering the pathway of one movement as it transits into the next movement, a dancer can find a way of traveling through movements by using their natural arcs and momentum paths. Once again, it must be emphasized that this type of flow is attainable only if the muscles work at their most efficient rate of contraction and decontraction. If the muscles around moving joints are unnecessarily engaged, the natural mobility of these joints will be hampered, affecting their range of motion and, therefore, their ability to respond naturally to the law of momentum.

When introducing dancers to the idea of momentum, it is useful to remember that the arms and legs can strike shapes that are angular and crisp. But the pathway in and out of these shapes will always be a curve. Acknowledging and using the momentum of curved movement is a key element in enhancing movement flow. Loops, arcs, overcurves, undercurves, spirals, figure 8s, boomerangs and tassels are only some of the rich images used in Hawkins training that bring attention to the beauty of this curved momentum flow.

FLOW AND TRANSITIONS

Because of its concern with organic movement execution, Hawkins training emphasizes the importance of cohesive movement flow and transitions. This does not mean that the shape and form of movement is less important. However, body shape and line alone do not make a dancer. It was Hawkins' belief that the movement and transitions between shapes and line are where dancing occurs.[52]

---

[52] In terms of flow and transitions, Hawkins felt a kinship with Isadora Duncan when she proclaimed that movement is in the *tran*sition rather than in the *po*sition.

Flow

The term "flow" is often used to describe the quality of a movement. For example, the movement of a river or a silk scarf suggests endless or seamless flow, while the movement of a piston or bulldozer suggests movement that is in some way effortful. These qualities of a movement's flow are determined, in part, by the degree and nature of force used in executing the movement. In dance terminology, movement flow is frequently described in relationship to a sliding scale of movement qualities; at one end of this scale is "free flow," at the other end of this scale is "bound flow."[53] If an otherwise integrated movement is uninhibited by tight muscles or by faulty initiation, the movement will have a quality of "free flow." If the same movement is executed with a large degree of muscular contraction, not permitted to extend to the full range of force applied to the movement, it is a movement that uses "bound flow." Because of its emphasis on achieving a sense of "effortless" movement and its attention to the transitions between movement phrases, the Hawkins technique is often described as being a "free-flow" dance style and "Hawkins" dancers are often admired for their fluid movement quality.[54]

As has already been mentioned, focusing one's attention on the transitions of movement rather than on the shapes and positions within movement affects the overall flow of a movement phrase. However, what is important to realize regarding flow is that it is merely a term used to describe the quality of a movement. By simply visualizing "free flow," a dancer/mover can perhaps succeed in achieving more fluidity through a movement. But, it is through the application of the concrete principles of

---

[53] "Free flow" and "bound flow" are terms stemming from movement research originated by Laban and are currently taught through the Laban-Bartenieff Institute for Movement Studies (LIMS) in New York City.

[54] Hawkins' "free flow" at its most poetic is evident in such dances as *Early Floating* (1961), *Classic Kite Tails* (1972) and *New Moon* (1989). Hawkins did not name his approach "free flow." He was very concise in stating that this was a Laban term used by many to describe his technique. However, he did feel that free flow was a larger idea of movement that encompassed bound flow in a way that bound flow could not encompass free flow.

think/feeling momentum, gravity and force that this freer flow can be most effectively accomplished.

Because of Hawkins' almost exclusive emphasis on free flow, as opposed to bound flow, the Hawkins technique is often perceived or interpreted as being a passive and introspective movement style. While Hawkins felt that freely flowing movement is more akin to nature and, therefore, in his opinion more beautiful, this emphasis on uninhibited flow does not preclude the possibility of highly dynamic and precisely formed movement that utilizes moments of efficiently executed bound flow.[55]

There is often a misconception that free flow lacks force. Quite the contrary is true. For example, a baseball player's swing of the bat will make the baseball go farther than if the bat was held still when it hit the ball. Likewise, a pitcher's free-flow throw through all joints allows for an explosive release of force, similar to the cracking end of a whip. In fact, this free-flow technique used by professional baseball pitchers can produce pitching speeds exceeding 90mph.[56]

The challenge of executing suddenly sharp and powerful movements requires from the dancer an even greater understanding of flow over the effects of brute force. When rapidly flowing water hits a rock, its flow does not stop, but rather it continues, immediately responding to the collision by changing its flow shape and pathway. In this same way, Hawkins maintained that free-flowing movement has greater flexibility to quickly change direction, shape or quality than does bound movement.

Hawkins continually emphasized that what constitutes a versatile dancer is the ability to execute a wide range of movement qualities. The

[55] While choreographing *Dazzle on a Knife's Edge* (1966), Hawkins made the conscious choice to explore his theories of movement efficiency and "free flow" within a highly dynamic movement vocabulary. Beginning with *Dazzle*, he began to use a full range of movement dynamics in all of his dances. For a further discussion of dynamics, see "Dynamics" in this chapter.
[56] James G. Hay, *The Biomechanics of Sports Techniques*, 4th ed., Prentice Hall, 1993, pp. 192–201.

The dance moves as a river from its source, as a spring in the Rockies until it flows into the ocean. Cathy Ward in *Greek Dreams, with Flute*, 1983.

DAVID FULLARD

dancer restricted by bound muscles resulting in bound flow has difficulty registering sensuousness or softness because the body lacks a necessary coenesthetic sensitivity and awareness. When accurately directed, free flow, on the other hand, is not only an optimal tool for evoking delicacy, but is also a powerful force for evoking strong movements. Although a dancer needs a range of ability at both ends of the free-flow/bound-flow spectrum, it is useful to remember that bound movement is not synonymous with power; nor is free-flow movement synonymous with inertness. Therefore, rather than being restricted by the limitations of muscle-bound technique, the well-trained dancer is able to choose from a wide range of dynamic expression between free flow and bound flow. The freedom of dancing in this way becomes, then, a metaphor for the dancer's free-flowing existence.

> Be
> as water is
> without friction
> > Flow around the edges
> > of those within your path
> > Surround within your ever-moving depths
> > those who come to rest there —
> > enfold them
> > while never for a moment holding on
> Accept whatever distance
> others are moved within
> your flow
> Be with them gently
> as far as they allow your strength to take them
> and fill with your own being
> the remaining space when they are left behind
> > When dropping down life's rapids
> > froth and bubble into fragments if you must

knowing that the one of you, now many,
will just as many times be one again
And when you've gone as far as you can go
quietly await your next beginning.[57]

FORM

A unique aspect of the Hawkins aesthetic is the way in which free-flow movement is carefully formed. Influenced by his study of ancient Greek thought and art, Hawkins spoke of form in the following way:

JOHN GERACI

There is a "classicism" in the world of nature and of art where form takes on a "violent clarity" that is utterly simple. Erick Hawkins in *openings of the (eye)*, c. 1958.

[57] Source unknown.

There is a "classicism" in the world of nature and of
art where form takes on a "violent clarity" that is utterly
simple, utterly without anything extra. After I had been
studying dance awhile, I knew that I had to find the
equivalent simplicity, clarity, and effortlessness . . . in
dance movement that I liked in everything else.[58]

In this love of simplicity and clarity, Hawkins shared an aesthetic kinship with such visual artists of his generation as Robert Motherwell,
Isamu Noguchi and Constantin Brancusi.[59] The way in which this simplicity of form affected Hawkins' explorations in technique is evident in
the sheerness and clear sparseness of body shape and line:

Everything is formed. That's why the idea of
raggedy clothes, or any kind of old music, or not
paying attention to detail is just dumb. Because the
whole point is how you intensify human pleasure
through form.[60]

This interest in form is connected with the idea that form has a distinct shape that electrifies and delights the human senses. The extreme
roundness and brilliant colors of the sun at sunset, a beautifully healthy
pine tree, the perfect triangular mound of Mt. Fuji in Japan: All of these
crystallize into a distinct form and bring pleasure to the senses.

A basic way in which Hawkins' extreme sensitivity to form manifested itself was in his attention to the details of the dance space and
dancer's physical appearance during class. Hawkins believed that the
simple formalism of a clean studio and the visible lines on the dancers'

---

[58] Hawkins, *The Body Is a Clear Place*, pp. 93–94.
[59] Brancusi, Noguchi and Motherwell were three of Hawkins' favorite visual artists precisely because of the clarity
and simplicity of their work.
[60] Erick Hawkins, Company Class, April 1985.

The simple clarity of a Hawkins studio, 78 Fifth Avenue, New York City, 1972. Nada Reagan Diachanko in rehearsal for *Classic Kite Tails*.

bodies, without jewelry or extra layers of clothing or loose hair styles, create an appropriate clarity and respect for one's work that directly affects the progress one can make as an artist. For him, the dancer is forever striving to make the body "a clear place." Therefore, within the challenges of enhancing movement flow, the dancer also works toward clearly articulating distinct form. Two examples of how this sense of form is enhanced during a technique class are the images of the "chalkline" and the "cobra hand."

The "Chalkline"

A chalkline is a string that has been dipped in chalk dust, used by carpenters to mark a straight line on a piece of wood for sawing. The string is stretched out over the piece of wood, then snapped back to

© DAVID FULLARD

The challenges of articulating clear form within movement flow. Daniel Tai as "Cloudcookoo-boro" from *Greek Dreams, with Flute*, 1983.

create the chalk mark on the wood. The Hawkins chalkline refers to an imaginary center line that extends into space directly in front of and behind the body, used to orient and shape arm and leg gestures.[61] For example, when lengthening the leg to the front or back, students are reminded to let the toes fall along this sagittal plane, directly in front of or behind the nose, along the "chalkline."

Using the chalkline image helps to orient the limbs along the central axis and assists in streamlining movement into the longest possible line of the leg and arm. The image also guides the arms and legs into distinct shapes. "Arbitrary" movement for Hawkins was movement that lacked a clear visual form. Therefore, shaping movement flow into a precise form

[61] The term "chalkline" probably originated with Isadora Duncan who first implemented an exercise she called "walking on the chalkline." It always refers to the horizontal extension of the vertical axis.

is an important element of Hawkins training that keeps free-flow movement visually clear.

"Cobra" Hand

The "cobra" image is often used to achieve certain arm patterns and shapes. Teachers use this image to encourage students to think of their fingertips leading the rest of the arm and spine into a movement, much like the distinctly rounded head of a cobra snake (see Figure 28). This results in an immediately curved arm shape in contrast to a more sequential arm pattern that emphasizes the tassel-like movement of the arm. Both are rich in their choreographic potential but involve a different arm coordination.

FIGURE 28.
The Fingertips as a
Cobra Snake

Normative Form and Aesthetics

Attention to creating clear form is a constant while learning basic classroom movement and choreographic repertory. Some of these shape-oriented details in a Hawkins class are the stylistic eversion of the foot during many leg gestures ("*sur le cou-de-pied*," as it is referred to in ballet terminology); emphasis on the parallel line of five fingers next to five toes (found most immediately in the Three 3s movement pattern); and the emphasis on a slightly lifted, buoyant elbow when the arm is extended to the side, referred to by Hawkins as a "winged" arm (for both, see "Three 3s" in chapter IV).

However, concern with form becomes a matter of stylistic choice, often going beyond the parameters of correct movement theory. For example, the everted foot, while a desirable finish to the line of the leg

Clear form and the "cobra" hand in Hawkins' choreography. Cynthia Reynolds, Mark Wisniewski, James Reedy and Cathy Ward in *Death Is the Hunter*, 1986.

The "*sur le cou-de-pied*" as an aesthetic choice. Barbara Tucker and Erick Hawkins in *here and now, with watchers*.

when the leg is lifted, is a potentially dangerous position for the foot in weight-bearing situations because the toes will tend to flair away from the center of a useful leg alignment. Therefore, when learning movement form, the dancer learns to recognize whether a movement form is derived from a technical premise or an aesthetic premise. In executing any form in any technique, the alert dancer bases his or her movement goals first on a technically

The buoyancy of a "winged" arm. Erick Hawkins in (*vulnerable male is magic*) from *here and now, with watchers*, c. 1962.

correct premise. Then, after the technical principle is mastered, it is possible to find a way of honoring a stylistic form according to the teacher's or choreographer's idea. Again, Hawkins would say that it is not that one movement is right or wrong; it is the way in which the dancer works within that movement that can be correct or erroneous (for a further discussion on form, see chapter V, "Beyond Technique: the Aesthetic Dimension").

WHAT IS RHYTHM? IS MUSIC SOUND?

Hawkins did not use music in class. It was a conscious choice made to encourage dancers to listen to and experience their own inner song and rhythm. During classes and rehearsals, Hawkins would continually stress the importance of being on the pulse of the movement, of obeying the rhythm of the body and of knowing the rhythmic structure of a movement. Beginning with the simple movements of the floor warm-up in class, students are encouraged to sense the body moving in harmony with these rhythmic elements at all times. When a dancer is in the immediacy of a movement's pulse there is a focus on the movement experience that translates into how the nervous system and muscles actually respond. Hawkins would often speak about the connection between rhythm and movement in the following way:

> Sometimes dancers have the illusion that the only way they can dance is to interpret the music. As though they have to be kicked in the pants by the musical sound all the time. And it's psychologically true that if you hear one kind of musical material, you start to move. Right? But if the dancer is activated only by hearing the sound, he or she is a little bit limited.
>
> The rhythmical vitality needs to be actually in the dancer's consciousness. When I say "sing," it's as though you were making your own music right as you do the movement. Sure, you're doing it in the pulse and meter that I happen to have set up for the moment—but once that's established, you're making your own phrasing and musical experience yourself.
>
> Actually, when we're singing a rhythm in the mind, it coordinates the muscles of the body. Rhythmic movement is the most efficient movement. Any movement that is not truly rhythmic in real pattern, starts to be mad, . . . alienated . . . disturbed . . . erratic. Rhythm is the very basis of the swing of life, from the sun and the moon, to the heartbeat, to all kinds of things like that.[62]

[62] Erick Hawkins, Company Class, April 1985.

Hawkins students are first made aware of rhythm through the sensing of musical pulse. The musical pulse of a movement is the perceivable regularity of how the movement progresses through time. It is the "heartbeat" of the movement: a consistently measurable unit of time.[63] Being "on the beat," as Hawkins would continually urge, involves shifting the majority of the body's weight in any given movement on this pulse. Hawkins continually created movement patterns with quick rhythmic weight shifts as a way of challenging his dancers to clearly articulate movement rhythm. As Hawkins' composer, Lucia Dlugoszewski, explains:

> There is a unique Hawkins recklessness and refreshing dangerous immediacy and sense of adventure in this challenge of shifting weight in time.[64]

Truly shifting weight on the pulse or rhythm of a movement creates harmonious and easeful kinetic flow. The challenge is to shift weight on the pulse. Often, when a student is off the pulse of music, it is an indication that he or she is not truly present in the movement experience. Interesting rhythmic structure can assist in taking dancers out of movement habit simply by challenging them to focus outside of the body on pulse and rhythm.

As class progresses, rhythmic sequences built from a steady pulse become more complex. Rhythmic invention can be created in one of three ways: Either pulses can be grouped into "meters"[65]; pulses can be subdivided into what Dlugoszewski refers to as "matras"[66]; or these subdi-

---

[63] Doris Humphrey, in her *The Art of Making Dances*, calls this the "motor" rhythm of a dance, pp. 105–7.
[64] Lucia Dlugoszewski, interview by Renata Celichowska, unpublished notes, September 21, 1999, New York City.
[65] The Hawkins "meter" equals a "measure" in music terminology.
[66] "Matra" is a word borrowed from Hindu music vocabulary by Dlugoszewski and Hawkins. Dlugoszewski believes in paying homage to the subtler use of rhythmic invention in Hindu thinking by using the word to express the "subdivision of a pulse."

visions can become dangerously obliterated from the pulse by consciously omitting or pulling off of the pulse, as in syncopation.

Hawkins used this sophisticated command of rhythmic pattern in order to liberate movement from the common trap of a predictable march or waltz rhythm. Rhythmic variety has become one of the hallmarks of Hawkins teaching. For example, in creating a movement pattern to warm up the feet, an instructor might use a combination that brushes from a parallel first position to the front, two counts out and one count in with the right leg, then two counts out and one count in with the left leg, then out and in on one count each with the right, then out and in on one count each with the left. The pulses in this combination are grouped in two meters of three, followed by two meters of two:

> 1 – right leg brushes out to point
>
> 2 – right leg continues to extend out through the pointed foot
>
> 3 – right leg returns to parallel
>
> 1 – left leg brushes out to point
>
> 2 – left leg continues to extend out through the pointed foot
>
> 3 – left leg returns to parallel
>
> 1 – right brushes out to point
>
> 2 – right returns
>
> 1 – left brushes out to point
>
> 2 – right leg returns to parallel

By using this type of rhythmic vocabulary, the dancer is able to clearly articulate a movement's rhythmic structure to other dancers or a composer without the confusion that usually ensues when dancers use "dancers' counts" (counts that do not use an even sense of pulse and that

Hawkins reading a score during orchestra rehearsal for
Plains Daybreak, 1982.

are not based on a logical system of music theory).[67] The challenge for the
dancer is to understand and then sing the rhythmic pattern through the
body. In this way the dancer becomes a skilled craftsman of time, being
able to use it and shape it in interesting and exciting ways. Hawkins in
his classes would describe this skill in the following way:

> Were you counting? Were you purring right with
> me all the time? When the mind is conscious very clearly

[67] Dlugoszewski in her well-known passionate style describes this shortcoming of many dancers as the "atrocious
illogic of dancers' ill-digested perceptions of time." (Dlugoszewski interview, September 1999.) Both Dlugoszewski
and Hawkins were aware that it is a failing and a dangerous handicap in much of dance training that dancers are
not taught to understand and use music theory more thoroughly.

of rhythm, the muscles of the body will show it. Many dancers think it just happens by itself . . . and it's true, we use a kind of intuitive sense . . . we hear something and we get an intuitive swing. But if you want to get into the lovely complexity of real "time" art, of either dancing or music, then the sophisticated dancer or musician will know what the rhythms are and embody them and make them more vivid. So, that's why you have to sing right along with the rhythm.[68]

This passionate love of rhythm translates directly into Hawkins choreography. Hawkins dancers are continually learning complex rhythmic structures of Hawkins repertoire that rarely follow the common 4/4 musical structures of many Western dance works. As a result, Hawkins choreography has an inherent element of rhythmic surprise and vitality that sets it apart from many other choreographic works.[69]

DYNAMICS

As stated before, the importance of creating form (such as distinctive shape and design) within flow is what prevents free flow from lacking aesthetic power. As Dlugoszewski describes the challenge:

> How can one sculpture something so ineffable as
> free flow? It is like catching the wind in a net![70]

The constant interplay between these two principles, flow and the forming of things, is one of the most exciting relationships in dance and

---

[68] Erick Hawkins, Company Class, April 1985.
[69] Two of the most extraordinary examples of this musical/dance marriage are the dances *Early Floating* (1961) and *Black Lake* (1969). All of the music and dance are woven together in time by the same metrical structure.
[70] Lucia Dlugoszewski interview, September 1999.

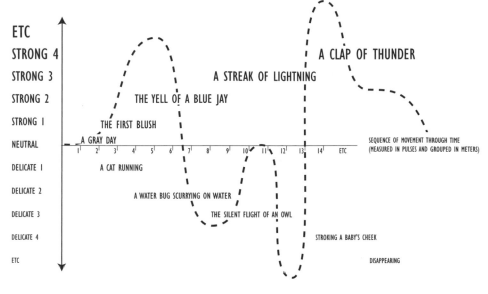

FIGURE 29.
Dlugoszewski's Dynamic Scale

is one that encompasses the idea of energy levels or *dynamics*. The use of dynamics in dancing predicates the aesthetic power of choice. A strong shape or angular form need not always be executed with bound flow, nor does free flow exclusively suggest subdued movement or shapelessness.

In teaching dynamics to dancers, Dlugoszewski devised a scale of energy-level gradations ranging from extremely strong to extremely delicate movements, similar to the forte and pianissimo qualities in music (see Figure 29).[71] The challenge for both the choreographer and performer is to clearly show the difference between the degrees of these strong and delicate dynamics and to be able to suddenly jump from one dynamic to another without graduated transitions.

In describing the power of using dynamics, Dlugoszewski lists the following images:

---

[71] Since the 1970s, Dlugoszewski has been sharing her theories on rhythm, dynamics and sensation in Hawkins choreographic workshops throughout the United States.

If a neutral dynamic equals a gray day:
Strong to the 1st power is the first Blush of Spring
Strong to the 2nd power equals the
    Yell of a Blue JAY
Strong to the 3rd power is a
    STREAK of Lightning
    or a Lion's ROAR
Strong to the 4th power is a pure
    CLAP OF LIGHTNING!

On the reverse end of the spectrum:
Delicate to the 1st power is a Cat running
Delicate to the 2nd power is a water bug
    scurrying on the top of water
Delicate to the 3rd power is the
    silent flight of an owl
Delicate to the 4th power is stroking
    a baby's cheek when he sleeps.[72]

As Dlugoszewski describes it, having a specific mental image for each dynamic of the scale gives the dancer a powerful language through which to speak to the audience.

When performing movement, the ability to oscillate between a strong, highly charged dynamic and a delicate, soft quality involves the sophisticated ability to contract and decontract muscles quickly. One of the distinctions of Hawkins dancing is the sudden transition from contraction to decontraction needed to shift suddenly to different energy levels.[73] For example, the choreography might involve leaping into the arms of a loved one whom the dancer then embraces. The ideal action of the muscles (if one was wanting to accentuate the tenderness of that

---

[72] Lucia Dlugoszewski interview, September 1999.
[73] See "Contraction and 'Decontraction'" in this chapter for a further explanation of this action.

moment) would be to change from the strong, muscular activity required in the leap to a quick decontraction of the arms, chest and face as the dancer experiences the immediacy of touch in the embrace.

Constantly changing dynamics is one of the exciting aesthetic elements joining Hawkins and Dlugoszewski. If one views and listens to a dance and score of their collaboration, this dynamic playfulness becomes quickly apparent. In Hawkins choreography one can notice the constant play of body shape and form, flow, time and dynamics. There are frequent contrasts and varying combinations between strong and delicate movement. The sudden change in dynamics surprises the eye and heart. As Dlugoszewski so often says, the idea is that at that moment of kinesthetic change in sensation, the dancer "gives the audience a flower."

IV. IN THE CLASSROOM

The basic format of a ninety-minute Hawkins technique class typically begins with what is called "floor work," progresses to a series of standing movement patterns in center and then, once the body is sufficiently warmed up, moves the dancer across the floor in traveling movement combinations.[74] However, it is important to emphasize that the Hawkins technique is not based upon a standard series of exercises. In fact, those familiar with either ballet training or Graham-based modern dance technique might recognize many familiar shapes. But knowing the movement patterns that Hawkins teachers give in the classroom does not comprise the full scope of the technique, nor was it Hawkins' goal. The crucial focus of Hawkins training is the ongoing investigation of movement principles: principles that are confirmed by objective kinesiological science and coupled with an acute sensitivity to the coenesthetic dimension of human movement experience.

---

[74] Hawkins at times also included barre work within portions of class as supplemental practice of form and precise body placement. He would also frequently mention that he thought the most useful format for class was to spend only 1/2 an hour on the floor, 1/2 an hour in center and 1/2 an hour moving across the floor.

Hawkins continually stressed that from the very beginning of class, the dancer was dancing, sensing, being alive and moving: moving with an aesthetic consciousness. In this sense, class for Hawkins was never just about warming up or toning the body. Although he believed in the daily practice of movement and was aware of the neuromuscular and cardiovascular requirements for an efficient warm up,[75] he did not believe in "codifying" movement forms. He believed that defining a movement form too rigidly leads to the disembodiment of that form from its life-giving movement investigation. A movement routine can quickly become automatic or "mechanical" (a word that Hawkins preferred to avoid in his discussion of movement). Human movement, while obviously containing many mechanical elements, also embodies a person's spirit. When movement becomes automatic, this spirit is often forgotten. An exploration of movement that emphasizes the mechanical aspects of the body without drawing attention to one's visceral response to the movement is no less dangerous than ignoring the mechanical facts altogether. Hawkins explained his attitude toward movement routine in the following way:

> Certain things which are very fundamental need to be done just so. When you are a finished dancer you still must do those certain movements. It is useful for professional dancers and student dancers to have some exercises that, regardless of whether they feel like it or not, they can do to warm up. Those habitual exercises will always prepare the person to dance. You need to inculcate correct habits. . . .
>
> [However], it is possible to codify the movement vocabulary with such stringent rules that it is utterly

---

[75] Most physical trainers and athletes recommend at least eight repetitions of basic preliminary movements while warming up. It takes at least eight repetitions of a movement to engage all of the muscle fiber in the working muscle.

dull. It has no adventure. This is always the problem of codifying anything. You rule out new possibilities. . . .

[Ralph Waldo] Emerson said, "People wish to be settled. Only as far as they are unsettled is there any hope for them.". . .

Today the dilemma is to not have too rigid a codification that will restrict the vocabulary of the student.

It is a constant dilemma to me, in running my school, whether I suggest that teachers follow what I find prepares the body for a class, whether I hold them to that, or whether I let the teachers make up their own movements. I have decided on the possibility of freedom.

That is what I mean by understanding principles. If the teachers make up their own movements (and I'm amazed and delighted with what they do), I know that they are doing them because they understand the principles I have taught them. If you do any movement by understanding the principle it will never be wrong.[76]

As Hawkins envisioned it, the task of the dancer is to remain continuously alive and sensitive to the natural needs of the body. If a teacher employs what Hawkins called the "poke and pull" method (where the teacher is physically manipulating the student into a visual facsimile of a desired form or shape), the dancer never gains a clear or useful coenesthetic sense of the movement. In this instance, the shape is something generated from outside the body rather than from an internal understanding and sensation of it. A dancer's awareness of his or her "coenesthetic sense" is, therefore, an invaluable tool in training. If a movement meets with muscular resistance, where is the resistance occurring? If the

[76] Hawkins, *The Body Is a Clear Place*, pp. 129–30.

upper arm or leg seems distorted, how can this distortion be corrected? These are the types of questions a dancer can ask himself or herself while working. Dancers who actively think/feel while they train are their own most effective teachers.

The following examples of common Hawkins movement patterns are included primarily to illustrate certain movement principles.[77] The floor warm up taught by many Hawkins-based instructors follows a general format that Hawkins typically used. Hawkins felt that these movement sequences were the most efficient forms through which to master certain movement principles. However, they are not meant to form a definitive codification of the "Hawkins Technique." As has been stated, Hawkins believed that there were countless ways in which these principles could be explored. Therefore, the student should be aware that the forms given in a standard Hawkins-based class can vary to a large degree and still be organized around common principles.

FLOOR WARM UP

Classes generally begin seated on the floor. The beauty of the floor warm up is that within the first half hour of class many of the principles forming the foundation for further movement exploration are introduced. By liberating the legs from their common weight-bearing function, students are given the opportunity to begin class with an experience of gravity and how it acts upon the body. Students are encouraged to sense the rootedness of the ischial tuberosities or "sit-bones" (also written as "sitz-bones"), as they are commonly called, as the weight of the upper

---

[77] See *The Erick Hawkins Modern Dance Technique Videos*, Parts I & II, for a complete illustration of the following movement sequences. The two 45-minute technique videos follow two Hawkins technique classes: a 1985 company class with Hawkins and a 1997 class with master teacher and former company member Cynthia Reynolds. The videos include interviews with Hawkins and archival footage of rehearsals and performances with the company.

body transfers through the spine and pelvis into the floor. This weight transferring into the floor is balanced by an equal force of energy extending up through the spine and out the top of the head.

Seated Movement Sequences

Throughout a Hawkins floor warm up, the importance of rediscovering the power of the body's center of gravity is continually reinforced. Movement impetus from the pelvis resonates through the spine into the rest of the body. In working toward maximizing movement efficiency and flow during class, students are encouraged to resensitize their kinetic and coenesthetic sense to the initiation of movement from this center. While seated on the floor, without the further complication of maintaining balance in a standing position, the dancer can concentrate on spinal integration and the power of flow that emanates from the center of gravity.

In a series of rockings or **bounces**, as they are commonly referred to in class, the spine lengthens and yields into a gentle curve, energy extending through both ends of the spine as the pelvis rocks over the heads of the femur bones (see Figure 30). All unnecessary tension is encouraged to release as a way of returning potential energy back to center. As energy con-

FIGURE 30. Initiating Movement from the Pelvis During "Bounces"

tinues to move out the top of the spine, the head and neck remain mobile and responsive to the initiation of the pelvis. The head weight stays within the loop of the rocking pelvis, without excentering into an overt whip to the front or back.

It is useful to note that the term "bounce" is somewhat of a misnomer. During a Hawkins "bounce" the spring or rebound in, say, the bounce of a ball is de-emphasized. Hawkins bounces stress a softer

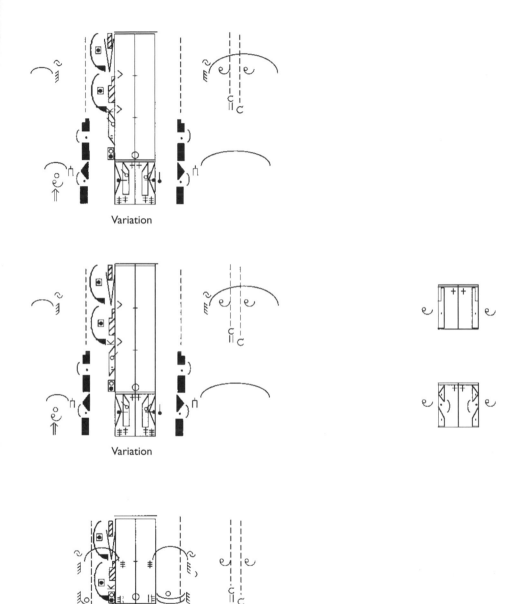

Variation

Variation

Bounces

approach. The gentle repetition of flexing and extending muscle allows the muscles and joints to fully warm up without the threat of injury that can occur when a more ballistic attack is used. For example, for this very same reason physical trainers perpetually discourage "tugging" at the calf or quadriceps muscles while preparing to run or exercise. The muscles need to be warm before they are required to stretch.

Variations of preliminary bounces and loops are possible in a number of forms. The pelvis can spiral to a diagonal facing over one leg. The legs can be placed out to the side or in a parallel front position. The arms can extend through a large number of loops and momentum patterns. Each variation of this simple rocking has its special challenge and offers tremendous information to the student about his or her movement range, energy consistency and central strength. As the pelvis continues to initiate and guide movement flow, other parts of the body go along for the ride. Much of the focus of this early part of class is upon getting in touch with this sense of initiation from the center of gravity in the pelvis and the continuity of its movement flow.

Side-lifts further challenge the student's integration and control of movement from the pelvis in an off-centered movement pattern. The name of this movement highlights its focus: One side of the spine lifts across the center line of the body (see Figure 31). Although the side-lift emphasizes the lengthening of one side, it is useful to remember that both sides of the body can lengthen and reach toward a higher vertical, similar to the

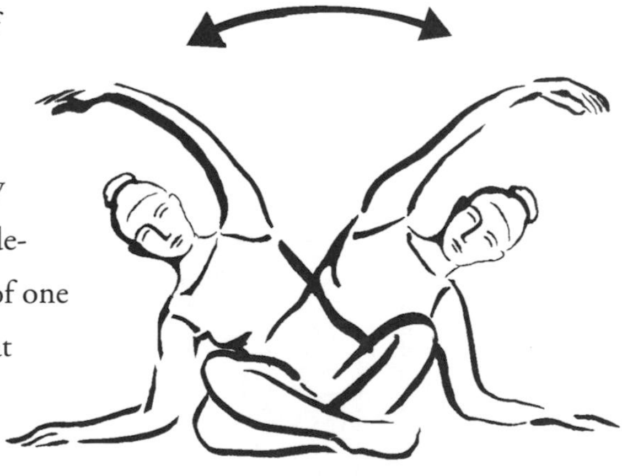

FIGURE 31. Seated Side-lifts

85

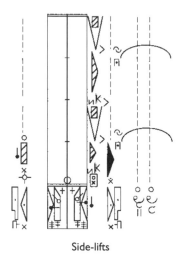

Side-lifts

way in which a fountain of water arcs up before splashing to one side. The spine reaches away from gravity, not down toward gravity. Some of the other ideas explored in this movement involve increasing movement range in the spine, maintaining a strong sense of groundedness through the floor of the pelvis and extending the central axis into a graceful and evenly arcing curve.

Examples of Side-lifts

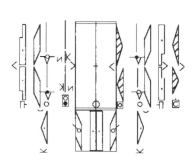

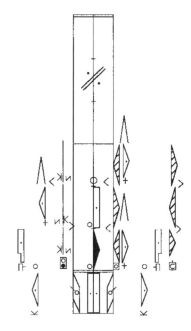

In order to achieve the richest curve in the side-lift, integration of the spine, head and limbs from the pelvis is essential. Students are reminded once again that the pelvic center of gravity is the root from which all other parts of the body extend. If one does not maintain a connection between one's center of gravity and the rest of the body, unnecessary muscular strain will occur, thereby binding movement flow.

When translated into standing movement combinations, a side-lift bending solely from the waist up cannot be integrated with the legs and arms without relying upon gripped muscles or distorted balance. Different body parts will be working at cross-purposes rather than all contributing to the kinetic purity of one movement. This does not mean that the shape always has to emphasize the same degree of side-lift; it simply means that the image of beginning the movement from the root of the pelvis has to be in the dancer's consciousness in order for the upper and lower parts of the body to work in harmony with each other. As described previously, the

structure of a starfish or the beautiful curves of a young tree trunk are vivid examples of this type of central integration. One of Hawkins' favorite images for the side-lift was that of a flower: The sit-bones reach into the ground like the flower's roots, the spine reaches into the sky like the stem of the flower reaching for the sun, supported on both sides so that the stem does not break.

As a primary movement of the spine, side-lifts form the basis for numerous movement

© JONATHAN ATKINS, 1988, NYC

The S-shaped arms of a side-lift. Michael Moses as "Eros" in *God the Reveller*, 1988.

phrases both in class and in Hawkins choreography. A generic way in which Hawkins formed the arms when responding to the side-lift of the spine is to allow them to find a natural curve. Using the arms in this way often results in an S-shaped arm pattern.

A **contraction-swing** variation of bounces introduces three-dimen-

sional flow through the spine as initiated from the pelvis. In a seated contraction-swing, the pelvis rotates toward the left (or right) thigh socket while in the C-shaped curve of the contraction (see Figure 32). The momentum created by the release of this pelvic and spinal spiral carries the pelvis,

FIGURE 32. Contraction-Swings

torso, head and arms along a forward arc that travels from a back left or right position, through forward center, and ends in a similar position on the other side. It is then either reversed or developed into other torso movement. The spine lengthens through a spiral as the head and arms tassel in response to the pelvis.

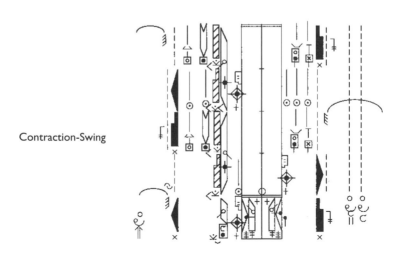

Contraction-Swing

A tendency in this movement is to let the upper body take over or excenter away from the pelvic initiation. The challenge is to allow the upper body, arms and head to respond fully yet remain connected to the pelvis. The use of spiral images through the spine and legs is a rich principle continually explored throughout class (see "Arcs, Curves and Momentum" in chapter III).

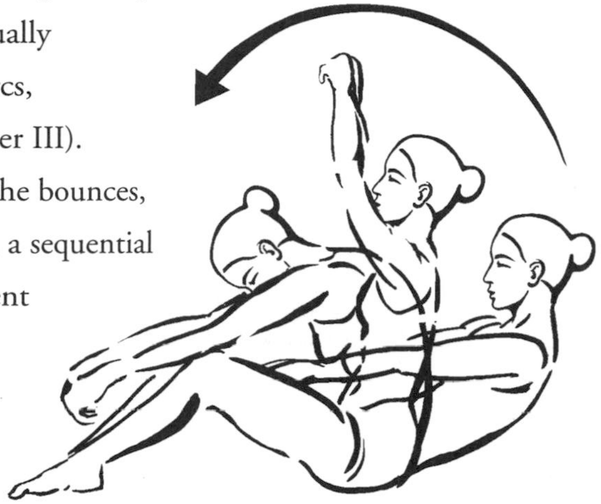

In an **overcurve** variation of the bounces, the spine responds to the pelvis in a sequential rather than simultaneous movement flow (see Figure 33). The challenge here is to allow the head and arms to tassel or respond in a sequential pattern to the pelvis without breaking the movement flow, either by a drop of the head weight in the back or a drop of the arm weight to the front. Emphasizing the continuity of sequential flow is a beautiful aspect of this movement.

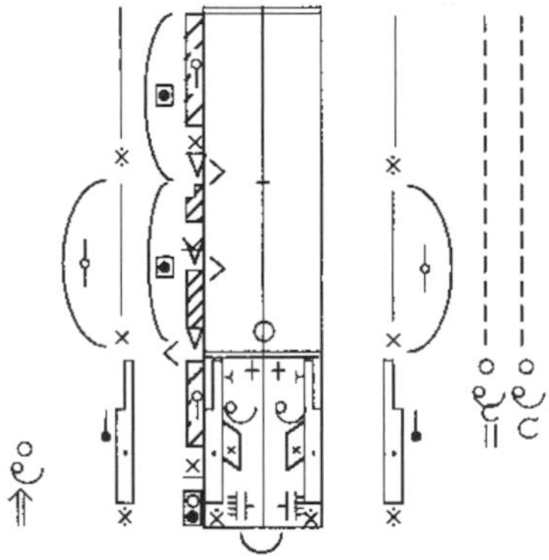

FIGURE 33. Seated Overcurve (Rippling Through the Spine)

Delight in the bare human foot was one of Hawkins' particular joys. In the seated overcurves, the feet are placed together in a parallel position on the floor with the heel, ball of the foot and toes yielding into the floor. Yielding the foot into the floor is a crucial element in balance and weight transfer that becomes increasingly important in weight-bearing situations.[78] Encouraging the toes, ball and heel of the foot to spread and respond sensuously to the

Seated Overcurve

[78] For a further discussion of footwork, see "Center Floor" in this chapter.

floor profoundly affects all further balance and movement suppleness. If the foot stays tense, the calf and shin contract, affecting the knee joint, which, in turn, sets off imbalances throughout the rest of the body. A sensuously responsive foot assists in the subtle shifts of weight involved in maintaining proper alignment and balance.

As stated previously, inseparably connected to the principles of main-

FIGURE 34. Lateral View of a Seated Contraction

taining balance through the body's center of gravity is the principle of muscular contraction and decontraction.[79] Similar to previous floor work, **contractions** focus on the impulse of power from the pelvis. In response to the initial impetus of the contraction (which can be thought of as an integration of the deep muscles along the front of the pelvis), the two ends of the spine lengthen and arc forward, allowing the front of the spine to yield back into center (see Figure 34). The degree of curve in the spine and position of the arms and legs in relation to the spine can differ to a large degree and still be considered a contraction. In its extreme example, a person can simply focus on contract-

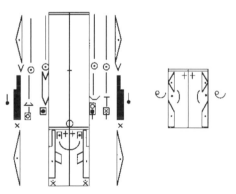

Seated Contraction

ing the abdominal muscles without encouraging any curvature of the spine and the movement would, technically speaking, still be a contraction. However, the word "contraction" as used in Hawkins training has

[79] See "Contraction and 'Decontraction'" in chapter III.

been extended from its original meaning of shortening muscular length to describe the resulting forward curve of the spine into a C-shape.

One of the beautiful challenges found in contractions is to continually yield all parts of the body back into center while engaging only the essential muscles. Hawkins often spoke of softening the sternum in order to achieve a three-dimensional curve during the contraction (curving both from front to back and from left to right). Yielding or decontracting the sternum against the strong impulse of the abdominal muscles involves a combination of opposing forces. Students are encouraged to allow the arms, legs and head to remain as decontracted as possible, coenesthetically connected to, but separate from, the strong contraction of the torso. In other words, the contraction of muscles in the pelvis does not necessitate the contraction of arm, leg and neck muscles. In fact, by allowing the entire body to participate in a contraction, the dancer actually halts movement flow. Again, if muscles unnecessarily contract around a joint, the movement and sensation in that joint is inhibited. As Hawkins would say, "Tight muscles don't feel!"

Contractions and other movements done with the legs extended to the side or to the front present the additional consideration of proper leg alignment. A series of **leg flexions** during a seated floor warm up reinforces appropriate leg action from the pelvis while the legs are in a non-weight bearing position. Whether in a parallel or turned-out position, students are encouraged to remember that the toes, ankle, knee and thigh socket work along a common axis. Deviation of one part of the leg from this leg alignment can cause serious injury when in a weight-bearing situation.[80] By taking the time to repattern leg alignment and coordination while on the floor, the risk of injury can be greatly diminished. Hawkins would often include a series of leg and foot flexions after contractions as a way of warming up and working on these leg principles.

[80] See "Leg Alignment" in chapter III.

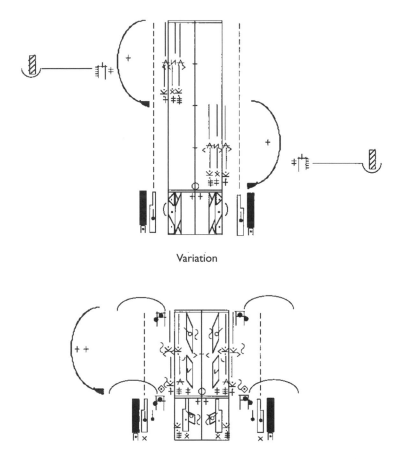

Variation

Point and Flexion of the Foot

Movement from what is called **fourth position** on the floor focuses on a deeper exploration of the spine as it spirals along more complex momentum paths. The name "fourth position" was adopted from the standing fourth position in ballet, which describes an asymmetrical position of the legs, one leg in front of the other. Similar to the Graham technique fourth position, a fourth position in Hawkins floorwork refers to a position where one leg is bent in front of the body and the other is bent behind (see Figure 35). The leg in front of the torso is turned out, all three joints fully flexed: The ball of the little toe rests on the floor; the heel is lifted up off the floor, reaching to the front along the chalkline; the

FIGURE 35. Seated Fourth Position

knee is directed out to a side/front diagonal. The leg behind the torso is turned in: The knee and thigh socket are creased, knee resting on the floor along a side/front diagonal; the ankle of the back leg is in plantar flexion resting on the floor.[81] Hawkins frequently pointed out that if correctly placed, the floor space described by the position of the legs forms a diamond in front of the torso.

One of the unique aspects of both the standing and seated fourth position is its asymmetrical orientation in space. It is a position where the spine has the opportunity to explore moving through all three planes of the body simultaneously: the horizontal (tabletop) plane, the sagittal (front to back) plane, and the vertical (side to side) plane.

Quarter turns in fourth position are a beautiful exploration of the balance of the three main weights of the spine, namely the pelvis, rib cage and head, as they spiral one sequentially after the other around a common vertical axis. The name "quarter turns" describes, in its most basic form, this quarter-turn spiral of the spine. The continuous curve of the spiral is often likened to the graceful pathway of a spiral staircase or the red and white stripes around a barbershop pole (see Figure 36).

---

[81] Plantar flexion of the ankle joint refers to a "pointed" foot position. Dorsal flexion is the equivalent of what is commonly called a "flexed" foot.

FIGURE 36. Spiraling Images for the Spine

In quarter turns, the pelvis, followed by the rib cage and head, initiates a lateral spiral of the spine toward the front leg and then returns along a similar path to its beginning position with both sit-bones on the floor, if possible.[82] Students are encouraged to focus, in their mind's eye, on the spiraling verticality of the spine as the movement travels up from the pelvis, through the rib cage and into the head. As the pelvis and spine participate in the spiral, the legs rest easily on the floor and the arms rest off the sternoclavicular joint along the front of the rib cage. The challenge for the arms is to rest on the air, without unnecessarily bracing or holding in a fixed position. Once again, rich images borrowed from ideokinesis are a poetic way in which to enhance the vitality of a still arm.

In its fullest form, the quarter turn incorporates first one arm, then both arms during its spiral. For example, if the right leg is in front, the quarter turn will move toward the right. While the spine spirals to the right, the right arm follows a path that travels through a forward center arc, passes over the head and then out to its right side. During the return-

[82] In Hawkins training, students are never encouraged to force the body into a certain shape or form simply for form's sake. Dancers are encouraged to challenge themselves as fully as possible within their own range of capabilities. Certain body types adapt more or less quickly to different movement forms. For example, resting both sit-bones on the floor in fourth position is often difficult for men, due to their narrower pelvic structure. Therefore, forcing the sit-bones down would most likely increase tension in many other areas of the body, which would work against a useful movement practice.

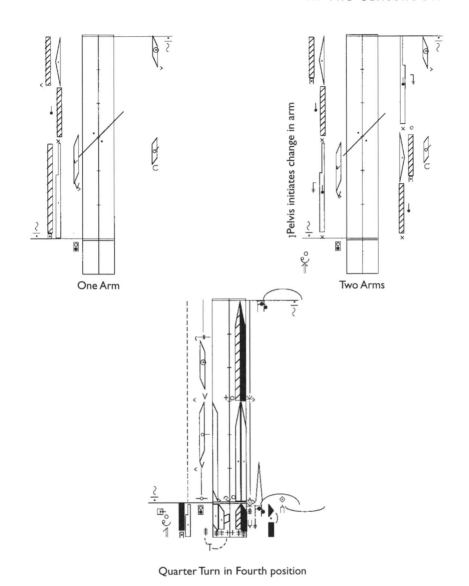

One Arm

]Pelvis initiates change in arm

Two Arms

Quarter Turn in Fourth position

ing spiral to the left, the left arm follows a similar path to the left while the right arm continues in a loop under and across the front of the torso (see Figure 37). When used in this way during quarter turns, the arms begin to describe a three-dimensional figure 8. A typical Hawkins image used to describe the sensation of the arm is to think of the arms as tassels, swinging loosely from a very actively integrated spine. Hawkins would

FIGURE 37. Figure 8 Arms in Quarter Turns

also often refer to the sensation of "mussing up your hair" as the finger-tips of the tasseling arms pass over the crown of the head. As class progresses, the use of the tassel image for the arms, legs and head forms the basis for many movement combinations.

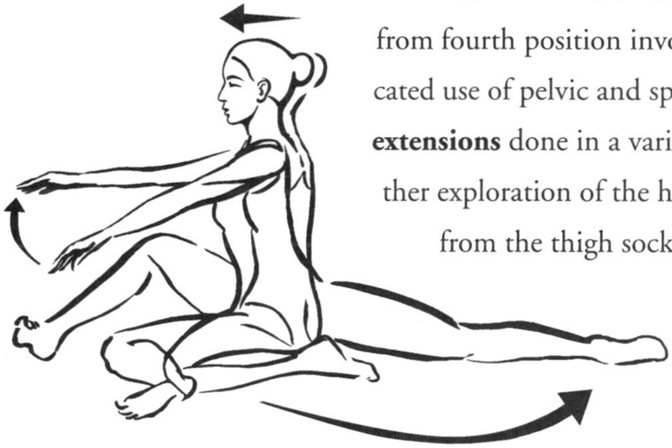

Additional movement patterns originating from fourth position involve increasingly sophisticated use of pelvic and spinal integration. **Back leg extensions** done in a variety of sequences are a further exploration of the hierarchy of leg control from the thigh socket. Students are reminded that the extension of a leg to the back begins not in the foot or knee, but in the pelvis. The subsequent spiral of energy initiated from center rotates the thigh socket out and continues to wrap around the thigh, the lower leg and foot (see Figure 38). The importance of being securely over the supporting thigh socket further prepares the student for later back leg extensions (or "arabesque" posi-

FIGURE 38. Back Leg Extension

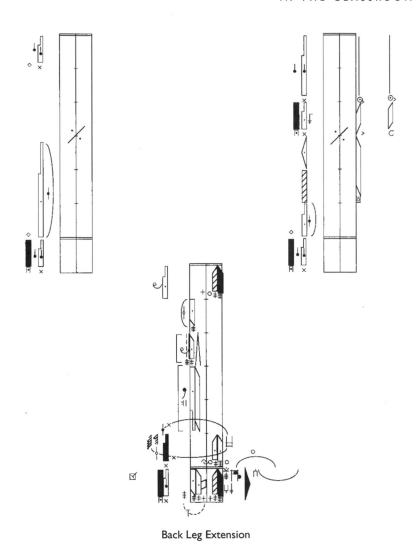

Back Leg Extension

tions, as they are called in ballet training) when standing. During a 1997 class, Hawkins dancer and teacher Cynthia Reynolds described the action of the leg in back leg extensions in the following way:

> I'd really like to see you clearly demonstrate the
> thigh moving away from the socket. So that again, we're
> using the hierarchy of the leg. It's not so much that the
> back of the knee opens, but that the thigh moves right
> out of the pelvis like a tendril off of a vine. . . . Really

KENN DUNCAN, 1972

Shift the pelvis and spine forward onto the thigh socket to find a secure and dynamic arabesque. Nada Reagan Diachenko and Carol Conway in *Classic Kite Tails*.

make that exquisitely clear in your thought preceding the movement.[83]

Three 3s,[84] also done from a seated fourth position, are a lovely movement pattern that highlights the sensations of contraction and internal spiral in asymmetrical forms (see Figure 39). As the pelvis initiates a contraction, the spine responds in a spiral that curves toward the back leg while creasing into the front thigh socket (1). The pelvis and spine then lengthen in a reverse spiral out of the contraction, into a hovering position over the front leg (2). Finally, the pelvis, ribs and head fall back in a reverse spiral contraction over the thigh socket of the back leg (3).

Maintaining a strong integration in one's pelvic center while the spine, limbs and head spiral and curve along these asymmetrical forms is

[83] Cynthia Reynolds, Company Class, June 1997.
[84] The name "three 3s" describes the rhythmic structure of the movement: three meters of three beats each.

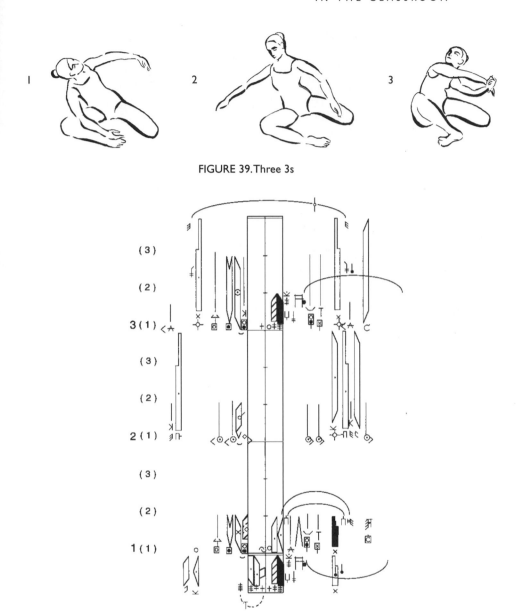

FIGURE 39. Three 3s

an invaluable aspect of this movement. Hawkins often used many poetic images when guiding students through the three 3s. Of special delight to him was the parallel relationship between the five fingers and five toes as the front arm rests along the front leg (in 1), and the sensation of later hovering over the leg, much like the way a mighty hawk hovers over the Great Plains (in 2).

The sensation of hovering over the legs like a hawk soaring over the Great Plains. Randy Howard in "Night Birds" from *Black Lake*, 1983.

A movement pattern called **swing on 5** (performed in five counts), is yet another exploration of the power of arcs and curves of movement as initiated from center.[85] In this form the legs, arms and upper spine are encouraged to act as complete tassels in response to the central attack of the pelvis. The moments of stillness before and after these impulses accentuate the dynamic tension between stillness and action. The directed swing of the arms through their gracious figure 8 pattern around center is one of the many challenges of this movement (see Figure 40).

Movement Sequences on the Back

A unique aspect of a Hawkins class is the time given to observe simple movement sensations while lying on the back. By lying supine on the floor, the body's relationship to gravity is beneficially altered, allowing the

[85] See *The Erick Hawkins Modern Dance Technique Video*, Part I, for a full illustration of this movement.

front of the body, the rib cage, muscles and organs to rest back toward the center line of the spine. Additionally, the muscles of the spine, pelvis, thigh sockets and legs, free of their weight-supporting function, have the opportunity to release and lengthen.

Many students come to Hawkins training with a large degree of unnecessary muscular tension. These dancers are initially challenged to change movement habits by simply feeling a softening or yielding of muscle. Prior to executing movement while lying on the back, Hawkins teachers often allow time for stillness, during which images of this softening or yielding into gravity can be incorporated into the body's coenesthetic sense.

The use of a modified "constructive rest" position, first implemented by Mabel Todd in ideokinetic work, is a typical position Hawkins used in his classroom

FIGURE 40. Swing on 5

1

2

3

4

5

(5)

(4)

(3)

(2)

(1)

warm up (see Figure 41).[86] The advantage of working from a constructive rest position is that all muscles and joints are in a relatively neutral position, requiring minimal muscular activity to maintain the position. The muscles around the heads of the femur bones and along the back of the lumbar and sacral spine have the opportunity to soften and yield.

Closely allied with this sensation of yielding is the sensation of releasing and widening along the muscles of the back. An ideokinetic image that enables students to release in this area of the body is that of two back pockets on a pair of pants sliding forward around the hips to the front of the pelvis.[87] This widening and releasing in the lower back is one of the most

FIGURE 41. Mabel Todd's "Constructive Rest" Position

healthful and helpful ways of protecting the lumbar and sacrum from undue stress and injury.

It is crucial to make the distinction here between the active sensation of decontracting or yielding in the muscle, and the passive collapse of muscle (see "Contraction and Decontraction" in chapter III). To enhance this idea of actively yielding, movement images of resting in warm sand or of sensing melting wax or of honey or water spreading along the floor are only some that a student might hear described during class. An ideokinetic image for this sensation is to imagine that you are a suit of clothing lying on the floor, experiencing air or sand passing out of the openings of the clothes as they settle on the floor.[88]

One of the key elements Hawkins training conveys to students is the sensation of a deep thigh socket integration joining the torso and the legs. Simple **thigh socket flexions** were one of Hawkins' favorite ways in

---

[86] For a description of the constructive rest position as used in ideokinetic work, see Sweigard, *Human Movement Potential*, pp. 215–21.
[87] Ibid., p. 239.
[88] Ibid., pp. 232–36.

which to promote an awareness of this area of the body. While lying on the back with the legs extended along the floor, the thigh socket initiates a slight flexion in one leg (see "The 'Thigh Sockets'" in chapter III). The tendency for many people during any kind of thigh socket flexion is to focus on the contraction of the quadricep muscles along the front of the thigh. The goal of this simple movement is to resensitize the body to the awareness that the flexion is initiated and controlled not by the quadriceps but by the psoas muscles.[89] As the psoas muscles are given an opportunity to regain their power as the primary flexor of the legs, the quadriceps have the opportunity to release unnecessary muscular tension, which tends to build unnecessary bulk in the legs.[90]

In a movement pattern called **rolling on 4** (the movement takes place in four counts), creasing in the thigh socket and yielding into gravity are explored further. Beginning with both legs lengthened along the floor, one knee creases up over the chest (usually done on a count of one). The pelvis then guides this knee into a roll across the torso, so that the front of the pelvis releases toward the floor with the trailing arm resting on the back of the lumbar (on the count of two). The pelvis then begins to tumble back into a soft lumbar spine, back onto the back, with the knee once again over the chest (on the count of three). Then the leg unfolds back onto the floor, the toes, ball and heel of the foot yielding and brushing along the floor (on the fourth count).[91]

Once again, the movement begins in the pelvis and thigh socket and

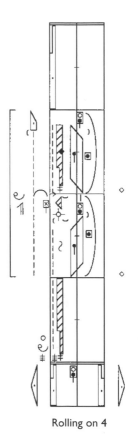

Rolling on 4

---

[89] See Figure 10, "The Iliopsoas Muscles" in chapter III.
[90] For a further illustration of this movement pattern, see *The Erick Hawkins Modern Dance Technique Video*, Part I.
[91] Ibid.

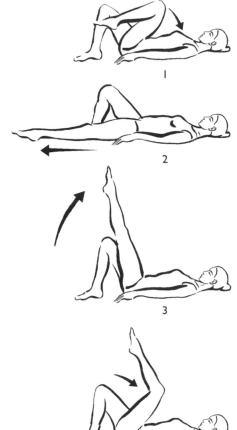

1

2

3

4

FIGURE 42. The "Boomerang" Leg

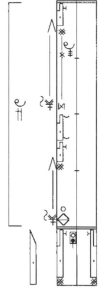

continues into the spine. The limbs respond accordingly, rolling through each position with a strong sense of weight and flow. Students are encouraged to control the tendency for the shoulders to take over the pelvic initiation and to continue to use free flow not as a passive collapse of weight, but as active momentum.

Further explorations of the generous movement range in the thigh socket evolve out of the initial thigh socket flexion. In what is termed a **boomerang** leg, students are introduced to the sensation of allowing the weight of the leg to fall back into a deeply creased thigh socket (see Figure 42). Beginning in the constructive rest position on the floor, legs in a parallel position creased at the thigh socket and both knees bent with feet flat on the floor, the boomerang leg swing begins with a creasing of the thigh socket. In response to this deep crease, the knee falls back toward the chest and the foot lifts up off the floor (1). From this position, the leg is then lengthened along the body's center line, traveling along the floor, away from the head (2). Using the momentum of this lengthening, the leg continues a loop that arcs through the body's frontal chalkline toward a vertical leg position (3). As the leg peaks within its vertical momentum, the challenge for the student is to then allow the momentum to act upon the leg joint, letting the leg fall back toward center and return to its fully creased position, with the knee resting back into the chest (4). This boomerang leg is, in some ways, simply a more specific use of the tassel leg, aimed toward encouraging a free-swinging momentum path through integrated leg alignment. Becoming acquainted with both tassel and boomerang leg images prepares the dancer for the subtle applications of momentum within more complex movement forms.

Once again, countless explorations of thigh socket creases, loops and boomerangs in parallel and turned-out positions are possible. The movement combinations stemming from these principles are tremendous and have a direct correlation to later movement involving the thigh socket when standing. Throughout movement sequences done lying on the floor, students are encouraged to continue using images of yielding into the floor, of feeling the tripod of the foot rooting into the floor, of using the least amount of effort and tension to execute the movement. The goals are ease and efficiency, which eventually give the dancer greater power and control.

Contractions while on the back reinforce many of the same concerns of the seated contractions. Students are encouraged to allow the head, arm and leg weights to rest back toward the center of gravity in the pelvis, decontracting unnecessary muscular tension in these areas (see Figure 43). The emphasis is on free-flow movement initiated by a strong impulse from the pelvis. Images that enhance movement flow, such as reminders

FIGURE 43. Contractions on the Back

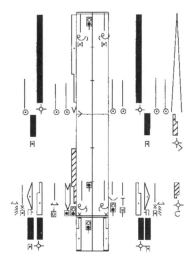

Contractions on the Back

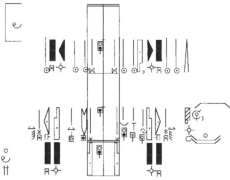

Contractions Rolling Up

of rhythmic patterns and continuous attention to the breath, prevent the contraction from becoming a static position rather than the vital initiator of movement. Think of the young branches of a tree as they bend under the weight of snow rather than break. Their suppleness, their yielding is what helps them survive.

Allowing for time to rock the pelvis from front to back and side to side is one of the many ways in which to enhance a feeling of widening and releasing in the back. A typical Hawkins class will often include a few improvisational minutes while lying on the back, when students are encouraged to wiggle the spine and toss the pelvis over the chest in order to release any excess tension in the lumbar and back of the sacrum. Hawkins would continually remind students of the merits of such a simple rocking movement:

> Now just rock the pelvis from side to side. . . . Every human being, the minute they get a little [physically] tired or psychologically tired and anxious, starts to tighten there, in the small of the back . . . and that's what leads to back trouble. So, I like to do this small movement in the pelvis so that it stops holding there.[92]

[92] Erick Hawkins, Company Class, April 1985.

A **figure 8** on the back is yet another exploration of the use of momentum and control of the center of gravity. The pelvis and lumbar resting on the floor act as the root from which the legs swing as tassels, guiding the knees through a figure 8 pattern.[93] Figure 8s are a marvelous movement through which to feel the difference between truly integrating a psoas flexion along the front of the pelvis and the unnecessary grip of upper and lower back muscles. The frequent tendency is to tighten in the lower back and/or attempt to stabilize the movement through added tension in the upper body. Instead, the body's weight can fall back toward center.

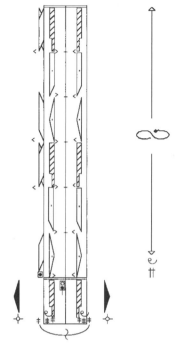

Figure 8s

Arching, or bridging the spine after thigh socket flexions, is an important release for the psoas muscles. The rippling sequence for the spine begins in the coccyx, progresses through the lumbar, thoracic spine and shoulders and then reverses back down from the neck and shoulders through the ribs, waist and pelvis (see Figure 44). The danger here is to unduly compress the vertebrae, especially of the lumbar spine. Students are encouraged to lengthen through both ends of the

FIGURE 44. Arching on the Back

spine. Although the pelvis bridges into a forward arc, the lumbar and thigh sockets are challenged to remain free and mobile. The rib and chest

[93] For a full illustration of this movement, see *The Erick Hawkins Modern Dance Technique Video*, Part I.

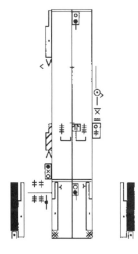

Arching on the Back

muscles need not excenter away from the thoracic spine, and the thigh and calf muscles in the legs need not unduly contract to stay balanced. As the legs bear more weight, students are reminded of the efficiency of a properly aligned leg, where the thigh socket, knee, ankle and toes work along a common axis.

Other forms of lengthening the psoas muscles are often used in class, including a gentle arching of the spine while on the stomach, or an opening of the entire torso to the side. Different teachers choose various movement sequences according to the needs of their students and the emphasis in class for that day.

Preparing to Rise from the Floor

Rolling off the back onto the knees reverses the pull of gravity on the body. In this transitional position, the weight of the body is supported by the arms and legs — an important precursor to transferring the weight of the body wholly onto the legs in a two-legged standing position. It is a wonderful position from which to feel the deep location of the thigh sockets as they begin to bear weight.

Reversing the torso into a stretch of the psoas, diaphragm and quadriceps prepares the legs for the gradual transition to weight-bearing. While lengthening the front of the extending thigh, the kneeling leg extends forward, while the back thigh, calf and heel lengthen back and up (see Figure 45). Students are encouraged to lengthen out of the lumbar rather than collapse into the lumbar toward gravity. If the rib cage is pulled too far back

FIGURE 45. Lengthening the Psoas and Leg

over the pelvis, the lumbar
vertebrae are put under
excessive strain, which can
cause serious misalign-
ment and injury in later
back leg extensions when
standing. Leg weight to
the back must be balanced
by a shift of torso weight
forward over the pelvis.

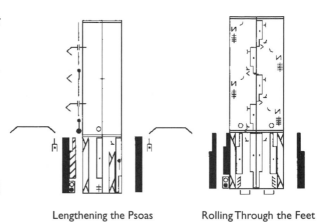

Lengthening the Psoas   Rolling Through the Feet

Gentle prances while on all fours (the "downward facing dog" position in Yoga) activate the feet, ankles and calves. Slowly, the focus of class
now begins to integrate the legs and arms more fully into larger movement forms. The goal of this brief stretching in class is not to encourage a
full-out stretch, which is more effectively and appropriately done at the
end of a class when the muscles are fully warm through cardiovascular
activity. Stretching or lengthening muscles midway through class is more
for loosening the leg muscles off a now warm center in preparation for
larger movement when standing.

Further exploration of back leg extensions can continue during **leg
lifts** done while on the knees. Due to the reverse pull of gravity on the
front of the pelvis, one of the
main challenges of movement
patterns from this position is
to maintain a sensation of
widening along the back of the
lumbar as the pelvis remains integrated across the front (see Figure 46). Students are reminded
to sense mobility in the lumbar

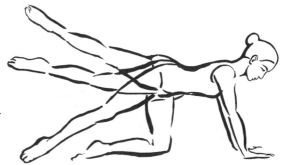

FIGURE 46. Leg Lift on the Knees

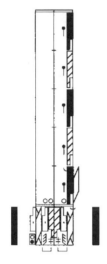

Leg Lift on the Knees

spine during leg lifts as they remain lifted up off the supporting thigh socket. This idea of letting the lumbar participate within a leg lift coincides with the anatomical fact that the psoas major is attached as far up the spine as the twelfth thoracic vertebra. Reminding students of this fact can enhance a sensation of length in the leg and its integration with the pelvis. Hawkins teacher Cathy Ward likens the mobility in this part of the back to the fluttering of butterfly wings. The sensation is light, quick, mobile and free.[94]

Rising to Standing

One of the most dramatic moments of weight shift during class is the transition from the floorwork to a standing position. It is normally the first time in class that the legs resume their full weight-bearing role and is, therefore, a critical moment to stay in one's think/feel sensation. The tendency in rising to a standing position is often to let the legs take over for the pelvis and spine. The goal of the rising ritual created by Hawkins is to avoid the loss of focus built during the floorwork, when changing to a standing position. Rather than get up "any which way," Hawkins believed in remaining sensitive to this radical shift in space, weight and alignment. Taking the time to experience this shift of weight and find one's efficient alignment through the spine and legs is an effective way to begin standing work (see Figure 47).

Beginning from a kneeling position, with the sit-bones resting on the heels, rising after a floor warm up involves rocking forward onto the

[94] Cathy Ward, Unpublished Class Notes, 1972. Hawkins soloist Cathy Ward has inspired many generations of Hawkins dancers with her poetic grace and expansive imagination. During the 1970s and early 1980s, Ward became the personification of the Hawkins aesthetic. Hawkins created many solo works for her, including her exquisite interpretation of "nymph of the grass and meadow" from the dance *Greek Dreams, with Flute* (1973), and the dynamically rich solos in the dances *Agathlon* (1979) and *Summer Clouds People* (1983). Encouraging lumbar movement should be tempered with a reminder that, when standing, stability of pelvic and leg alignment is a first priority. If the student becomes "locked" in the habit of overemphasizing lumbar movement at the expense of a useful pelvic placement in, for example, a front leg swing, then the torso will tend to collapse into the pelvis, the pelvis will tend to "tuck," added pressure will be put on the front of the quadriceps and the movement of the leg will be restricted.

hands and knees, allowing the toes to flex under the ankles (1). The weight is then transferred back to the thigh sockets and heels while the body remains rounded over the front of the legs (2). As the weight transfers into the thigh sockets, knees and ankles, the legs now resume their weight-bearing func-tion. It is an ideal oppor-tunity to experience gravity act-ing upon this weight transfer through the legs. While standing in a rounded position, knees bent, the weight continues to transfer back into the heels, causing an increased gravitational

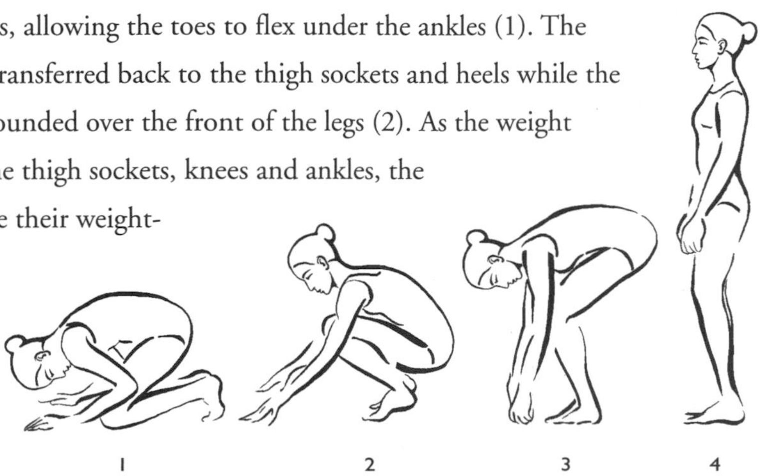

FIGURE 47. Rising to Standing

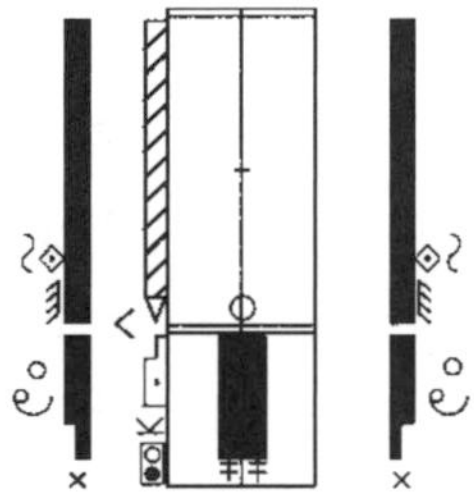

Rolling Up to Sitting

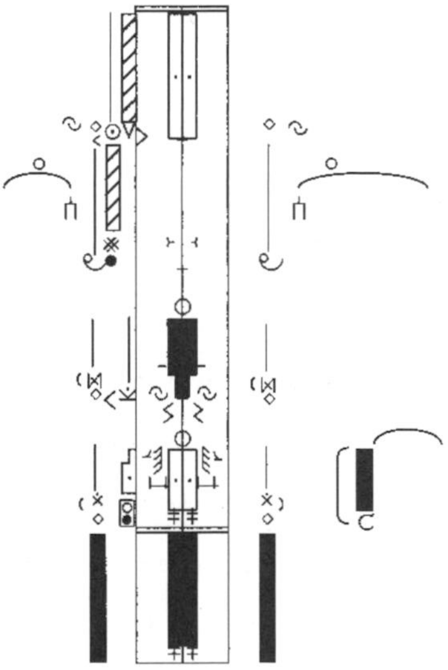

pull through the plumb line of the leg joints (3).[95] Once securely balanced through these lower joints, the student continues to rise by tracing the journey of each vertebra, beginning from the lower spine through to the superior (uppermost) end of the cervical spine, as the vertebrae stack, one on top of

Rising on 4

the other, toward a lengthened vertical axis (4). As the spine unfurls, the joints of the legs straighten so that all parts of the body reach their full verticality simultaneously. Instructors encourage students to allow their

[95] The plumb line of the leg joints is the vertical line along which the weight of the leg travels. When the thigh socket, knee and ankle joints are optimally aligned in a creased, standing position, this plumb line will travel through the center of all three joints.

spines and leg joints to remain sensitive to changing weight and balance, without reverting to postural habits upon which they might usually rely.

CENTER FLOOR

The floorwork is designed to provide the student with a basic vocabulary through which to understand the language of more intricate movement sequences. As class continues after the floor warm up, all elements introduced on the floor find fuller expression in increasingly complex movement patterns.

A standard Hawkins class usually progresses after the floor warm up into a series of simple "center floor" patterns, allowing the dancer sufficient time to warm up the legs and feet and re-establish a sense of the upper body's balance over the legs. By lifting from one's center during all standing work, the beautiful sensation of balancing on the top of the thigh sockets is a think/feel coordination that greatly affects the placement of the legs, pelvis and spine. Rather than allowing weight to sit in the thigh sockets, the dancer can think of the teeterbabe, of a buoy floating on water, of only one angel dancing on the pinhead of the femur bone. The legs remain active, yet loose and responsive, like a wasp with its strong center and dangling legs. As class expands into faster and more complex weight shifts, pelvic integration over muscular control of the movement by the legs plays an increasingly crucial role in achieving clean and smooth transitions.[96]

Pliés

Knee bends, or "pliés," as they are called in ballet technique, are a direct and simple way of beginning any standing work. Taking the time

---

[96] See *The Erick Hawkins Modern Dance Technique Video*, Part II, for a full illustration of teeterbabe and the effects of lifting from the pelvis.

to warm up the leg joints properly is crucial in preventing unnecessary injury. A useful idea to keep in mind during pliés is that the movement initiates and occurs in the pelvis and thigh sockets, not just in the joints of the knees and ankles. Thinking of lowering and lifting the pelvis and softening through the hierarchy of properly aligned legs takes undue stress away from the knees and ankles. Hawkins often observed that pliés are part of a universal movement vocabulary:

> [Pliés] are human movements in use all over the world. The Watusis use big pliés in the 2nd position of ballet terminology; the Cambodian dance uses predominantly 4th position; the Bharata Natyam of India, the oldest tradition of dance in the world, uses 3rd position of ballet as its preliminary position. All movements that can be used afresh are incorporated into comprehensive dance training.[97]

A number of images based on Hawkins' ideas for pliés are poetically used by Cathy Ward, including the following:

> Delicate pliés. Guide the knees out. Shift easily through the transition between the inside of the pubic arch so as not to tilt the pelvis. In the mind's eye, water trickles down the back and the coccyx. Guide your knees out while you trickle down your coccyx. Pay attention to pulse in metered patterns—feel—SING—demonstrate your real sensation of pulse![98]

Endless variations of pliés with added side-lifts, contractions and arm patterns are possible. As stated previously, forms introduced during the

---

[97] Erick Hawkins, Gail Myers interview.
[98] Cathy Ward, Class Notes, 1972.

floorwork become the basic vocabulary from which to build additional movement phrases. However, the principles remains the same: Initiation of movement begins from the center of gravity in the pelvis; energy travels up, weight transfers down the central axis; the farther away from center, the greater the challenge to control from center. All these factors are technical principles governing all movement patterns.

Sensuous Feet Against the Floor

The grounded connection of the body to the floor, first felt through the sit-bones while sitting, is now sensed through the feet. As explained earlier, sensing the feet on the floor is a delightfully immediate tool that offers the dancer continual information regarding balance, placement and force. Using the counterforce of the feet resting into the floor against the lift of the pelvis out of the legs is a dynamic approach to lengthening the entire leg. The foot needs to be strong, yet supple and sensitive.

There are many images that can be used to encourage an appropriate use of the foot against the floor, enabling a teacher to take into account the needs of the student. Some teachers emphasize the "tripod" of the foot, which is formed by the heel of the foot, the ball of the big toe and the ball of the little toe. The tripod image assists in stabilizing the foot, which helps to avoid over-pronation or supination of the leg.[99] The tripod also relates to the image of weight transferring through the instep across a system of two bridges, one starting from the ankle joint and descending into the heel and ball through a longer, sagittal arc, and one arching along each side of the foot along a shorter, lateral arc. Yet a third image is to think of the foot as an "arrow," with the stem of the arrow beginning at the heel and the arrowhead being formed by the ball of the big toe, the ball of the little toe and finishing out the tip, between the second and

[99] For a further explanation of pronation and supination, see "Leg Alignment" in chapter III.

third toes. Whether a teacher emphasizes resting more into the heels or using the ball and toes more depends upon a student's habit of using the feet. The goal is to keep all sensation alive in the foot.

Preliminary foot brushes along the floor ("tendus" in ballet) warm up this smooth and sensuous action of the foot. In any standing work it is useful to sense the weight of the pelvis and upper body lifting up off the legs while allowing the toes, ball of the foot and heel to yield into the floor. Meanwhile, in the brush, the articulating leg is encouraged to swing freely. The thigh socket, knee, ankle and toes all work along a common axis in a hierarchy of leg movement.

Principles Expanded

Dancing is flow. Within the demands of creating form, all movement is enhanced by honoring this basic fact. Explorations of the sensation of teeterbabe and weight shift expand after simple brushes. Interesting rhythmic patterns or surprising dynamic changes can become the focus of yet another movement sequence. The emphasis of an unusual form or body shape can be the inspiration for an additional combination. As movement becomes more complex after the initial floor and standing warm up in center, all of these principles become increasingly unified by the overarching challenge of being aware of and masterfully using efficient movement flow.

After basic pliés and foot brushes, a class can proceed in an endless variety of ways. The following points are based upon principles explored during a 1985 company class with Hawkins (see *The Erick Hawkins Modern Dance Technique Video*, Part II). They in no way encompass all the many elements of complete training. They are presented here as only one illustration of how basic movement principles expand into a useful movement vocabulary for the comprehensively trained dancer.

Using the Thigh Socket Crease and the Boomerang Leg

Similar to the thigh socket flexions on the back, the challenge in a standing thigh socket crease with boomerangs and brushes is to maintain mobility and ease in the legs. An example of such a movement sequence is as follows[100]: While standing in a turned-out position on one leg, the free-swinging leg brushes to the front and then loops and bends on its return past the other knee into a straight-legged position to the back (see Figure 48). Some of the details of this type of movement are that both legs remain lengthened until the apex of the brush, when the boomeranging momentum causes the legs to begin their return; the standing leg softens into a bend and the brushing leg loops past the standing leg and lengthens through the chalkline into a back leg extension.

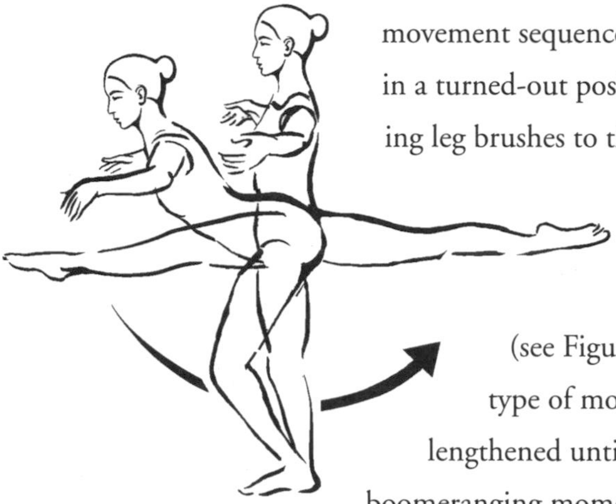

FIGURE 48. A Standing Boomerang Leg

The goal of a movement pattern like this is to not accentuate the straight gesturing leg at the expense of overly contracting the back muscles, tightening the knee, gripping the toes and basically halting all sensation of flow in the leg. Using the chalkline image to clearly place the gesturing leg; remembering to integrate along the front of the pelvis as the leg lengthens to the back; allowing weight to travel through the plumb line of the spine and standing leg—these are just some of the many principles upon which a student can focus during this type of boomerang leg sequence. Hawkins comments on this movement:

> Now let's do a brush. . . . It's not going to be very
> high. Let's do it so that it's on the chalkline and the foot

---

[100] See *The Erick Hawkins Modern Dance Technique Video*, Part II, for a complete example of this particular movement pattern.

is everted. That foot has a beautiful curve, like the end of
a pagoda in Bangkok where the roof comes up. It exists
just for pure aesthetic pleasure. It doesn't have to be
there. It's just a pleasurable action . . . but it's not simply
decorative . . . it's much more meaningful than that.[101]

Moving the Pelvis and Upper Body Together Through Space

As class begins to travel more in space, the important integration of
the pelvis with the upper body becomes more evident. One dangerous
pattern for students when they first turn their total attention to the pelvis
and its power is that they often forget that the rib cage and head are two
additional major weights along the vertical axis that need to move in
conjunction with the pelvis. As Hawkins often explained in class:

> A very good place to think of transferring the
> weight is to fall up here [pointing to the sternoclavicular
> joint]. The second place where you can think of going
> forward is right at the thigh socket . . . so that the ster-
> num is always falling forward OVER . . . over what? . . .
> Yes . . . , over the thigh socket—think of going over
> both—the thigh socket and the stepping leg. You're get-
> ting over [onto the leg] and not behind it. That [being
> behind the leg] is what makes it look like someone is
> reluctant to go on—or stuck.[102]

Thinking of all parts moving in tandem during a movement is a constant image with which to work. A frequent Hawkins reminder would be
to think of the "pelvis and spine first and let the legs follow for great technique," or one can simply think of "taking all bones into the direction
you are moving."[103]

[101] Erick Hawkins, Company Class, April 1985.
[102] Ibid.
[103] Cathy Ward, Class Notes, 1972.

Turns and the Spiral Staircase

In executing turns, Hawkins teachers frequently use the image of the spiral first introduced during the floorwork. In what is called a spiral staircase turn (referred to as a "fondu"[104] turn in ballet technique), the dancer concentrates on the sensation of weight descending as if down a spiral staircase, while softening and turning from a straight-legged, half-toe position into a full-footed, bent leg position (see Figure 49). Using this spiral staircase image of weight transfer through the legs contributes to the smooth ascent and descent within a turn and assists in maintaining turn-out from the top of the thigh socket down through the heel of the foot, preventing a dangerous inversion of the knee or sickle of the ankle. An important aspect of using the spiral staircase image is to maintain a sense of verticality around which the spiral can wrap. Shifting the weight of the body through an overcurve onto the supporting leg allows the longest vertical descent possible.[105]

FIGURE 49. The Spiral Staircase (Descending Through the Leg)

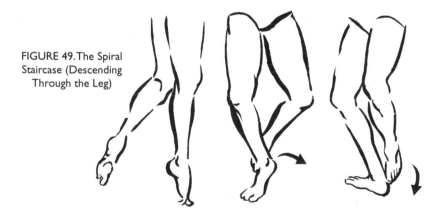

---

[104] The English translation of the French word "fondu" is "to melt," implying smooth descent during these types of movements.

[105] See *The Erick Hawkins Modern Dance Technique Video*, Part II, where a variation of this basic spiral staircase is illustrated. Instead of descending from the ball of the foot through the spiral staircase into the heel (which is a more standard use of the spiral staircase image), the dancers in the video practice a spiral that ascends from the heel of the foot to the ball. However, in both cases the pelvis and spine shift onto the standing leg through an "overcurve."

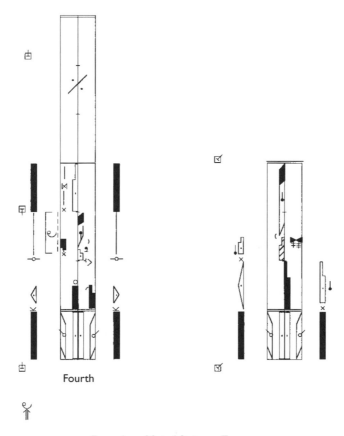

Fourth

Examples of Spiral Staircase Turns

Letting the Movement Happen: Staying in Coenesthetic Experience

"Let the movement happen, let the movement find its own rightness. Pay attention to the coenesthetic experience of the movement. Use your think/feel faculties." Hawkins was famous for these and his favorite exclamation of "just do the movement!" Only by staying in our senses are we able to stay in correct movement. In this sense, our bodies are our own best teachers. Hawkins often said that teachers never really teach anyone anything. They merely present information and ideas. The student teaches him- or herself. This recurring theme of Hawkins training — the reawakening of a dancer's ability to recognize, perceive, sense, experience and trust universal principles — offers a wealth of information from which even the most advanced dancer can continue to learn. Hawkins dancer and teacher Nada Diachenko says that the beauty of Hawkins training is that once the technique coalesces in the body, it stays in the body's sense memory.[106] All that is required to cultivate this sense memory is attention. As Hawkins said many times:

> We're in movement all the time. We're in correct movement all the time and we go out of it at our peril. Obviously, the real result of being out of the laws of movement is that it finally results in injuries.
>
> Sure, if you're trying something for the first time, you're apt to not quite be able to get feedback or a sense of it. So, every once in a while one hurts oneself. . . . For example, if you're doing some special carpentry, every once in a while you might jam your finger because you're thinking of something else. But, in general, when one injures oneself, similar to the carpenter, it's because you're not paying attention to just the way it works.[107]

Staying focused and paying attention to the way a movement feels and to "just the way it works" offers a lifetime of challenges for dancers of all abilities. This is the beauty of staying alive in one's own sensual experience of the dance. In its fullest manifestation in Zen philosophy, practicing full movement consciousness becomes a walking meditation that can encompass every waking hour of the day. In the technique class, the dancer has the opportunity to experience this type of movement focus from the very first step into the studio through to the very last leap out of the studio.

---

[106] Nada Reagan Diachenko, interview by Renata Celichowska, unpublished notes, 1987. Former Hawkins soloist and master teacher Nada Diachenko became one of Hawkins' primary partners during the 1960s and early 1970s and continues to teach his principles in universities and private studios throughout the United States.
[107] Erick Hawkins, Company Class, April 1985.

TRAVELING

When traveling across the floor in movement combinations, both a teacher's and a student's individuality is most clearly expressed. A Hawkins teacher might choose to work on movement from company repertoire, movement from his or her own choreographic project or simply movement that has evolved out of the focus on one principle in class. A student might be interested in focusing on rhythmic accuracy, continuity of flow, dynamic range or any variety of other movement challenges. Each class has its own tempo, mood and objective for each individual.

However, from a technical standpoint, traveling through space is a challenging test of the dancer's integration of *all* of these many principles. For example, the principles of the under- and overcurve of the pelvis can be explored in a simple "grapevine" (side-back-side-front) traveling pattern across the floor (see "'Under-curves' and 'Overcurves'" in chapter III). While traveling left, the weight shifts to the left in an overcurve onto the left leg, then shifts through an undercurve as the right leg crosses back, then over as the weight shifts to the left again, and under again as the right leg crosses front. This side-over, back-under, side-over, front-under pattern is a simple combination used by many Hawkins-based instructors that effectively tests a student's mastery of a number of basic principles. Among the many concerns of this movement are the under- and overcurve weight transfers of the pelvis and spine, the teeterbabe support of the pelvis, the clear articulation of the thigh sockets as they soften into the undercurve and the supple use of the feet against the floor.

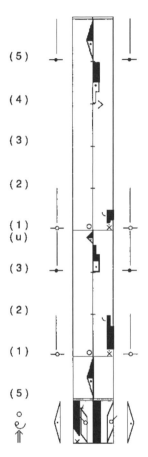

Examples of a Traveling
Combination

A simple combination such as this can then be embellished with other elements practiced earlier in class, such as the side-lift of the torso and/or the cobra use of the fingertips and arm. Beginning with a basic movement pattern and later developing it by adding turns, leaps or other choreographic elements is a useful teaching technique implemented by effective teachers of all dance styles. If developed in a logical and interesting way, this "simple-to-complex" teaching format promotes a student's thorough experience and understanding of the fundamental principles of even the most complex movements.[108]

Use of the Dance Space

In addition to carefully choosing and developing movement combinations for class, Hawkins was very conscious of the way in which he used the dance space during class. Two typical ways in which he used the dance space during traveling combinations were: 1) across the upstage half of the space, from stage right to stage left, and back across the downstage half of the space, from stage left to stage right,[109] and, 2) from the upstage to downstage diagonals, beginning from upstage right (see Figure 50). It is interesting to note that Hawkins made the conscious choice during the 1960s to begin all traveling combinations from the right side of the dance space moving toward the left. As former company member Penny Shaw explains it, Hawkins wanted to move away from the tendency to always generate and practice movement on his dominant, right side, in an attempt to more fully balance the body both physically and creatively.[110] He, therefore, chose to invent movement that either moved onto or toward his nondominant, left side, first.

---

[108] Hawkins would generally repeat a movement sequence at least once before developing it further, allowing dancers time to experience it fully in their bodies.

[109] Using the dance space in this type of "racetrack" formation keeps the momentum of the class going because the nondancing time for each dancer is minimized. While one group of dancers crosses along the upstage portion of the space, another group can cross from the other side, along the downstage space.

[110] Penelope Shaw, interview by Renata Celichowska, unpublished notes, August 1999.

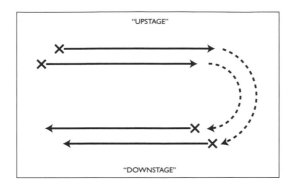

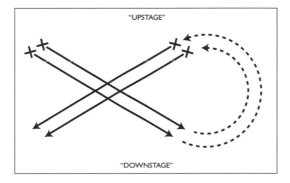

FIGURE 50. Using the Dancing Space

Moving directly across the dance space while generally facing down-stage offers a number of unique movement opportunities. By using a turned-out position, many fast foot combinations can be explored because of the ability of the feet to quickly shift from side to side from this position. The fast pace of a light and quick traveling foot combination across the floor is also an excellent way in which to build up a cardiovascular workout prior to any large jumps. As practice for dancing on a proscenium stage in performance, movements that begin and end along the sides of the dancing space prepare the dancer for entrances from and exits into theater wings.

Practicing traveling movement combinations along the diagonal of a dance space offers its own set of advantages and challenges. Practically speaking, moving along a diagonal gives the dancer the longest traveling space possible. In many studios this is the only way in which large leaping sequences can be practiced. Moving along the diagonals of a space also challenges the dancer to clearly articulate three-dimensional form by using facings ("*épaulement*" in ballet terminology) and focus effectively. Finding a useful balance between being in profile and facing forward is one of the obvious signs of an accomplished dancer.

One frequent oversight of dancers working primarily within the four walls of a studio space is that they forget to send their energy out beyond the limits of their own kinesphere, beyond the limits of their own image in the mirror, beyond the limits of the room's four walls, beyond the limits of their city. If a dancer does not practice letting energy project outward in the classroom, then his or her energy will not project outward in the theater. How will that dancer be able to touch someone with energy if that energy never projects beyond three feet? Regarding focus and attention, Cathy Ward relates a story about a hot day in class with Hawkins:

It was a hot day in the middle of the summer . . . and Erick suddenly backed up to the far side of the room and simply said, "Remember what's Eternal." Wow! It was such an amazing moment.[111]

Vertical Space, Jumps and Leaping "Over the Moon"

One of the most exciting elements of traveling through space and taking space includes claiming vertical space in jumps and leaps. Jumps are also a time when dancers are most likely to revert to inefficient kinesthetic coordinations. A useful principle to remember is that the degree of buoyancy at the top of a jump is directly affected by the power of integration from the pelvis at the beginning of the jump. Therefore, the primary

[111] Cathy Ward, interview, August 1999.

Jump with a buoyant lift in the pelvis and let everything else go along for the ride. Katherine Duke in *Cantilever II*, 1988.

factor in achieving the breathtaking height and suspension of a jump or the "over the moon" arc of a leap can be achieved only by initiating the jump from a powerful center of gravity. No degree of pushing from the legs will create a buoyant jump if the center of the body's weight (in the pelvis) is not actively propelling the movement. When frogs or cats or any kinds of jumping animal prepare to jump, they nestle back into their thigh sockets, gathering the whole of their body's weight back into a compact center before springing forward. The most efficient way of tossing a spool of yarn or a sweater is to collect it into a tight ball. Use the buoyant lift of the teeterbabe image as a source from which to toss the pelvis. If the power of the jump comes from the pelvis and the teeterbabe image, the legs, arms and head can easily dangle and go along for the ride.

Typical tendencies that work against a soaring jump and smooth landing from a jump include: 1) relying too heavily on the leg muscles;

2) pushing forward in the back of the neck at the top of the jump; and
3) keeping the muscles of the foot contracted and overly tense during the
landing. Overly worked quadriceps without an integrated center make for
a stunted and strained jump; a tense neck pulls the weight of the head,
and subsequently the entire upper body, forward and down; a gripped
foot causes brittle landings and can cause serious injuries in the foot,
ankle, shins and calf muscles. Ride the buoyancy of the pelvis, release the
neck and head up and out of the jump, yield the foot into the floor on
the landing. The momentum created by a well-integrated takeoff and
landing will make the jump feel and, therefore, look "effortless."

A simple leaping phrase Hawkins frequently used to promote correct
jumping patterns was a basic run-run-leap combination performed on
four counts, alternating sides. For example:

1 run right
2 run left
3 leap
4 land right
1 run left
2 run right
3 leap
4 land left

Although this basic pattern can be performed in countless ways,
Hawkins would frequently emphasize the "up-over-the-moon" quality of
the pelvis within either a single bent-leg or double bent-legged position
for what he called an "antelope" leap.[112]

---

[112] The "antelope" leap is illustrated in *The Erick Hawkins Modern Dance Technique Video*, Part II. It is a version of
this leap that is used in Hawkins' choreography for the beginning of the dance *Plains Daybreak*.

Ending Class

During a well-balanced ninety-minute technique class, Hawkins-based technique instructors aim to guide students through an adequate warm up (both on the floor and standing), a few simple movement combinations that can be easily repeated and more complex combinations both in center and traveling through the dance space. These goals are, of course, very generally stated and manifest themselves very differently according to the personality and interest of each teacher.

A class might finish with a fast movement combination across the floor, with a simple movement pattern in center or with group or individual stretching. The movement possibilities are endless. If a class does not end with stretching, students should be encouraged to stretch on their own after class, while the muscles are warm. This type of regular stretching after a cardiovascular workout can go a long way toward maintaining healthy muscle tissue and preventing injury.

Each class is a different experience for the teacher and student. This is the beauty of the immediate experience—of being in the NOW, in class, in live performance and in every moment of life. The dancer strives to make the body a clear place: a clear place without movement eccentricities or limiting idiosyncratic habits. Hawkins believed that awakening both the dancer's physical and aesthetic sensibility was a part of gaining this clarity. It was his belief that understanding and practicing universal movement principles in the technique class leads to greater skill and freedom as an artist onstage. But technique is only the beginning of complete dance training.

V. BEYOND TECHNIQUE:
THE AESTHETIC DIMENSION

Consideration of the aesthetic dimension in Hawkins training returns to Hawkins' basic premise that "nothing is ever separated from any other relationship in the world."[113] In this sense, what a dancer or choreographer finds technically desirable or aesthetically beautiful is born out of a fundamental philosophy of life. Therefore, in his teaching, Hawkins never isolated technical training from its aesthetic aspect or from its place within a person's life experience. For Hawkins, learning theoretically and aesthetically were inseparable. Hawkins felt that from a dancer's first dance class and through an entire dance career, both the theoretical and aesthetic aspects of the craft needed nurturing. Comments similar to the following were typical during Hawkins' classes:

> Once you've obeyed the scientific laws of movement,
> there is another aspect . . . the *aesthetic* dimension. And
> that is where the artist comes in. I don't care if it's a folk
> artist . . . it could be the way the Japanese arrange a little

[113] Erick Hawkins, Gail Myers interview.

dish of salad. There is another place where you go beyond just what is practical or utilitarian. . . .

And so, when you use that word "aesthetic," it is the basis of what we mean by BEAUTY. And why something is beautiful is something people have always argued about.

My feeling is that you can see in art from all over the world, of all periods . . . all the way from the cave paintings on . . . that there is something in the human spirit, in the human culture that has gone into the aesthetic dimension. . . . Human beings have always made art! . . .

[A]nd so, probably one of the most important things that would need to develop in American education is simply that children at the same time that they were learning, hopefully, to read and hopefully to learn arithmetic and so forth, also would have their aesthetic sense awakened. Because it can be daunted.[114]

This persistent reminder of the aesthetic dimension in life coexisting with the scientific dimension of life, of the inseparability between body, mind and soul, elevated the study of dance technique with Hawkins to a profound experience of artistry and life. A person makes choices every minute of the day in how they dress, speak, play and work. Technically there may be only one truth as to how to execute a movement safely and efficiently. However, aesthetically there exists an infinite variety of choices as to how to form that movement. A choreographer makes certain choices regarding the elements of a dance, such as movement sequences, shapes, timings and formations. These choices reveal his or her originality.

The way in which Hawkins manifested his "imagination of form" was through his interest in the simplicity and clarity of design; in the

---

[114] Erick Hawkins, *The Erick Hawkins Modern Dance Technique Video*, Part II.

contrast or introduction of the "disparate element"; in his highlighting of asymmetrical body shape and group form in space. Having come to these aesthetic preferences and choices on his own, Hawkins eventually discovered that he shared an uncanny kinship with Eastern and Zen aesthetic thought. Hawkins and many Zen-influenced artists believed in what Belgian existentialist Harvey Rochlein called the "Theater of Perception."[115] Hawkins wanted to strip art to its essentials and base his art on immediate experience, resulting in a concrete poetry similar to the artistry of classical Eastern poets. In dance, this meant choreographing and performing in such a way as to heighten the audience's perception of the pure beauty of the moving body, which, regardless of whether or not the dance was to express an additional idea beyond the primary beauty of the movement, remained Hawkins' foremost goal.

F.S.C. Northrop and the 1st and 2nd Functions of Art

Hawkins explained the distinction between "pure" movement and more narrative, thematically-based movement by using the powerful aesthetic insights of Yale philosopher F.S.C. Northrop. Northrop's aesthetic thinking profoundly mirrored the insights of Hawkins and his colleague Lucia Dlugoszewski. In his writing on aesthetics Northrop made the differentiation between what he called "1st Function Art" and "2nd Function Art." Art in its 1st Function, as Northrop defined it, is art that utilizes the raw materials of its form to convey nothing beyond the sheer sense of wonder of those elements.[116] For example, in painting, the colors and textures of paint can be composed to express nothing other than the simple beauty of their colors, shapes and patterns. A streak of blue paint across the top of a canvas means nothing more than a streak of blue paint.

---

[115] Harvey Rochlein, *Notes on Contemporary American Dance*, University Extension Press, Baltimore, 1964.
[116] F.S.C. Northrop, *The Meeting of East and West*, The Macmillan Company, New York, 1946, p. 407.

PATRICK BENSARD

1st-function dances delight in the wondrousness of movement elements. Douglas Andresen in *Agathlon*, 1980.

Hawkins' obsession with the concreteness of pure movement is an example of his love for art in its 1st function. His 1st-function dances use dance elements such as body shape, sensation, time as duration or rhythmic variation, dynamics and the flow of movement to express nothing other than the excitement and wondrousness of seeing the beautiful human body delighting in those elements. Some of his best-known 1st function–inspired works are the dances *here and now, with watchers* (1957), *Early Floating* (1961), *Cantilever* (1963) and *Cantilever II* (1988).

For Northrop, at the other end of the spectrum from art in its 1st function was art in its 2nd function, which uses the raw materials of an art form to convey a meaning beyond the scope of the materials themselves.[117] Instead of simply being a blue streak of paint across the top of a canvas, the blue becomes sky and sky carries with it all of the metaphors and/or images inherent in our perception of sky. Hawkins dances that emphasize art in its 2nd function include *John Brown* (1947) (revived as *God's Angry Man*, 1985), *Parson Weems and the Cherry Tree, Etc . . .* (1976), *The Joshua Tree* (1984), *God the Reveller* (1987) and *Killer of Enemies* (1991).

[117] Ibid., pp. 407, 486.

2nd-function dances express an additional idea beyond the movement elements themselves. Erick Hawkins in *The Joshua Tree*, c. 1984.

In between these two extreme ends of the 1st and 2nd function spectrum exists a full range of art works that use a varying degree of metaphor or story, where the raw elements of an art form are used to "suggest" an image or poetically express a metaphor for something. Some of the dances in which Hawkins uses poetic metaphor in a non-narrative dance include: *Lords of Persia* (1965), *Black Lake* (1969), *Classic Kitetails* (1972), *Hurrah!* (1975), *Plains Daybreak* (1979), *Summer Clouds People* (1983) and *New Moon* (1989).

Movement vocabulary in all of these dances, regardless of whether or not they are 1st- or 2nd-function dances, emphasizes poetic gesture and the use of movement metaphor, and not, as Hawkins would say, a "naive-realism" of pantomimic gesture. For example, in the dance *God the Reveller*, the death of the character Dionysius is portrayed through a duet between Dionysius and the figure Death, dressed in a simple black tunic and mask. Death silently enters and holds out his hand. Dionysius slowly takes it. After an almost lyrical interchange between the two men, involving a quiet pushing and pulling of the arms, Death quietly overcomes Dionysius and lowers him to the ground, assisted by the character Sleep. Dionysius wears no overwrought facial expression, nor is there any overt movement choreographed that pantomimes killing or dying. Instead, the struggle between the two characters is portrayed through movement that becomes a metaphor for death. The dramatic narrative progresses poetically, not realistically.

The "Hawkins Aesthetic"

For Hawkins, beautiful movement in all of his dances was the result of moving effortlessly, with a wide range of dynamic and rhythmic play. Many of the movement phrases Hawkins discovered for his choreography were the result of classroom explorations of principles. Conversely, Hawkins would often bring to class movement ideas for his choreography. The interplay between technique class and the creative process was constant. A dancer versed in the standard vocabulary of Hawkins technique will recognize many principles and movement forms from classroom practice in Hawkins repertory.

For example, in the dance *Agathlon* there are many instances when the hand is directed along the path of the chalkline or used with a cobra hand initiation (see chapter III). In both *Classic Kite Tails* and *New Moon*, Hawkins made extensive use of side-lifts and figure 8 tassel arms, principles that emphasize the curved movement flow of the dances (see "Side-lifts" in chapter IV and "Loops and the 'Figure 8'" in chapter III). In the dance *Black Lake*, Hawkins carefully etched body shape and rhythmic structure. For example, in the duet "Night Birds," the dancers emphasize the winged shape of the arms practiced in the three 3s, and in the solo "First Star," the dancer must rely on impeccable alignment when executing the dance's many challenging leg extensions. In the fast-paced solo "Comet," the continually changing metric structure of the dance is a rhythmic tour de force for the soloist.

Simplicity and clarity of form is perhaps one of Hawkins' foremost aesthetic statements. Hawkins repertory is governed by a sheerness and economy of movement that is much like a Brancusi sculpture or Motherwell painting. Nothing is extraneous or left unconsidered. The dance *Black Lake* evokes the setting sun, the first star, the moon and clouds, the Milky Way and other elements of the evening sky with an unadorned minimalism that heightens every gesture with poignant immediacy. The carefully chosen movement gestures in the duets of *Early Floating* etch the unadulterated vulnerability and sensuousness of the interaction between the dancers. The choices Hawkins made regarding the minimalism of his costumes, sets and lighting were all conscious decisions. He aimed to emphasize what he called the "violent clarity"[118] of form.

Another distinctive element of the Hawkins aesthetic is his use of the disparate element. A disparate element, upon first glance, seems set apart from the world of a group of elements. But its strangeness is exactly what creates a surprising accent and mystery. For example, in the dance *8 clear places* (1960), Hawkins chose to accent the simple, needlelike mask and dark tunic for his "Pine Tree" solo with a red sleeve. Nothing about the sleeve or its red color would normally signify "pine tree." But it is the contrast of this sleeve against the rest of the costume that adds a unique statement to the work.

In movement, Hawkins often added the disparate element of an unusual shape to an otherwise standard movement. For example, in technique class Hawkins would often use a simple "chassé"[119] movement

[118] See Hawkins, "Questions and Answers," in *The Body Is a Clear Place*.
[119] *Chasser* is a French term meaning "to chase," used in ballet vocabulary. It describes the universally used galloping movement of many dance styles.

pattern embellished with a quick tassel of the arm or change of direction. During pliés he would frequently add an unusual torso facing or arm gesture. The disparate element of a surprising rhythmic change was one of Hawkins' favorite challenges. He would often alter the rhythmic ending of a movement sequence by shortening the metric phrase. Hawkins technique classes use this same rhythmic structure. Seated contractions are normally executed on the count of 3 and finished with a forward release on the count of 1. The three 3s are normally executed on the count of 3 and finished on a count of 2. Even while practicing these basic movement principles in class, Hawkins would look for the aesthetically exciting.

Hawkins repertory includes a wide range of disparate elements in movement shape, tempo, rhythm, dynamics and flow. In the dance *Classic Kite Tails*, there is an extensive use of angular or sudden arm gestures that contrasts with the overall lyrical qualities of the dance. These momentary shimmers of shape and speed keep the dance dynamically charged. During the opening of the dance *Today, with Dragon* (1986), Hawkins added the intriguing element of small pieces of painted wood, hand-held by each dancer, purely for their aesthetic playfulness.

Asymmetry both in Hawkins training and in Hawkins repertory is another prevalent feature of the Hawkins aesthetic. The asymmetry of the side-lift, of the three 3s, of odd metered rhythmic structures, of unusual movement sequences that emphasize an off-centered shape of the torso, arm or leg — all of these elements emphasize the exciting beauty of asymmetry.

Hawkins' asymmetry in choreography can been seen in the design of body shape, in his organic use of group formations and in his choice of costuming and set design. The entire premise of the dance *Agathlon* is based upon the precarious asymmetry between imbalance and balance inspired by the unique rock formation of the same name in an Arizona Navajo Reservation. All of the movements and group formations, the cos-

The sensuous asymmetry of costumes. Laura Pettibone in *Summer Clouds People*, 1983.

tuming and set are explorations of asymmetry, from the opening fall and rebound of the one dancer juxtaposed against the other seven to the barely perceptible costume changes, to the elegantly poised sculpture stage left, to the final repetitive jump of the male dancers punctuated at the end by the emergence of a solitary female figure. In costuming, Hawkins would continually delight in the dynamism of asymmetrical design. The simply designed tunics for the dance *Summer Clouds People* feature the sensuousness of one bared shoulder and one covered shoulder. They are neither kimono, sari nor toga. They are their own world of beauty.

Simplicity, clarity, disparate element, asymmetry: These are only some of the details that shape the Hawkins aesthetic. But to truly understand it one must experience it in all of its immediate vulnerability. Short of that, perhaps the only other way to evoke a picture of Hawkins and his unique movement poetry is by listening to his own thoughts on the subject. After all, the Hawkins aesthetic is and will always be Erick's. When asked what he considered to be the most beautiful dance, Hawkins replied:

Dance that is violent clarity.

Dance that is effortless.

Dance that can at all times reveal a tender breastbone.

Dance that lets itself happen.

Dance that dedicatedly loves the pure fact of movement.

Dance that knows the most beautiful and true movement
    starts in the pelvis and spine and flows in the tassel-like
    legs, arms and head.

Dance that uses technique that is an organic whole, not a
    grab bag of eclecticism.

Dance that does not stay in the mind, even the
    avant-garde mind.

Dance that senses itself instant by instant.

Dance that loves gravity rather than fights gravity.

Dance that has reached such a height of subtlety
    it can stand still.

Dance that loves time, time as a sensed duration,
    and all the subtle asymmetrical divisions of time,
    and yet always the pulse of time.

Dance that never ignores, either audience or music or
    stage or fellow dancers. Therefore, no frozen faces.

Dance that does not try to explode the same bubble
    twice. Neo-Dadaism being exactly that: the already
    exploded bubble.

Dance that is not a sheer shambles and general mess, a new
    Dada, anything goes, throw it together, kid stuff.

Dance that is grown-up, composed by post-adolescents
    for post-adolescents.

Dance that knows soundness in psyche and body always
    produces rhythmical movement; that spastic and
    catatoniclike movement is illness.

Dance that knows movement and music put together
    without a common pulse is two people talking to
     you at the same time. Something is ignored!

Dance that knows you must have live musicians as well as
    live dancers or you have dead music and dead theatre.

Dance that knows the longer recordings are used, the longer
    it will take us to find the correct music for dance.

Dance that is aware of what a woman is and what a man is.

Dance that knows how to show that the love of man
    and woman is neither soupy nor misery.

Dance that reveals the dance and the dancer.

Dance that knows that the art is more than the personality
    of the dancer.

Dance that uses virtuosity only in the services of 'poetry,'
    not as acrobatics misconceived as art.

Dance that does not separate sacred and profane.

Dance that knows dance is a metaphor of existence.

Dance that can paraphrase the ancient Hindu saying,
    'Let those who dance here, dance Him.'

Dance that knows dance is, should and can be a way
    of saying now.[120]

Dance Education and the Role of the Dance Teacher

Although Hawkins was concerned first and foremost with his artistic life, his deeply rooted belief in the importance of art and dance in nurturing a healthy spirit was integral to his work. In addition to running his school in New York[121] throughout his entire career, Hawkins was also

---

[120] Erick Hawkins, *The Body Is a Clear Place*, pp. 38–39.
[121] The Erick Hawkins School for Modern Dance was founded in New York City in 1951. Teachers from this school continue to train dancers throughout the world. It is one of the oldest schools of modern dance in the United States.

committed to performances, workshops and lecture-demonstrations for children. In speaking about his work for and with children, he would often describe the joy and excitement he felt in witnessing them experience their own aesthetic awakening:

> [During our Seattle tour] we did two performances back-to-back every day for two weeks for sixth-graders in the Seattle Opera House. We were performing for 12,000 kids in two days! That is a creative act! Now I don't give a hoot about the fact that it was me or my work. But, I was showing those children the works of two dances that had been commissioned from two of our most beautiful American composers. And for me to talk about that in a curtain speech . . . and for those children to hear and be conscious of our American composers, I think that is right!
>
> I think that the reason that dance, in terms of human culture, is so important, is that it works with the prime instrument of our actual existence, which is our carcass, our body-hyphen-soul.
>
> As the young learn to find correct movement, it actually helps their cell structures develop properly. So, the reason behind getting children to see the dance is simply to give them a normative ideal of how human beings can move. And ultimately, then, by their seeing the image of correct movement according to nature and kinesiology, hopefully intellect and imagination will tell them what would be the most life-giving way to proceed in their lives. . . .
>
> The development of our correct movement can really lead to this development of a totality. Dancing in terms of an image of human activity is not in any way separated from intellectual or emotional balance. They

are all necessary for the whole . . . and if you can get this
to the children, then, why of course, its wonderful![122]

Art and education for Hawkins were inseparable. One was essential
to the other, much in the same way that he believed that aesthetics and
technique exist side by side. Aesthetics brings life to technique and education. Education and technique bolster aesthetic expression. And, as
Hawkins so often stated, it is only through the fulfillment of both of
these aspects that dance can become a metaphor for an artist's existence.

[122] Erick Hawkins, Gail Myers interview.

VI. HAWKINS CHOREOGRAPHY

Although the focus of this book has been on the technical contributions of modern dancer Erick Hawkins, the aesthetic vision he championed for more than forty years is a crucial aspect of his life's work. The following is a compilation of his choreographic works, presented in chronological order according to their premiere dates.[123]

From the cut of the costume on the dancer's body to the quality of craftsmanship in the set, to the clear tones created by a violin or piccolo, to the sensitively designed light on the dancers, Hawkins believed that all aspects of a dance work were equally important. Hawkins always worked in close collaboration with his composers and visual designers and had a strong influence on the final outcome of each of their contributions.

Hawkins was completely committed to new music and live music for each of his dance works. Even in the exceptional cases when he choreographed to pre-existing music,[124] all scores were composed by twentieth-

---

[123] This is the first time that a chronology of Hawkins' works has been published. Therefore, information is still being researched and confirmed for accuracy.

[124] The dance *Classic Kite Tails* (1972) was inspired by American composer David Diamond's *Rounds for String Orchestra*. The dance *Greek Dreams, with Flute* (1973) used solo flute works by Debussy, Varèse and a number of other composers.

century composers and were always performed live by the Hawkins Theatre Orchestra. This is how Hawkins described his commitment to new music and live music:

> When I work with a composer it's as though he's my other self writing it. And we may or may not succeed. But we're trying to find our own vitality right in our own culture. . . . You cannot have a new statement in dance unless you have a new statement in music. . . . If I'm really watching the human spirit come to a high point of immediacy onstage and I hear some old ideas in the music, for me there is a schizophrenia about it. That old music, if I am sensitive, will make me dance in the flavor of what that is saying. I can't be my own minute-by-minute contemporary self when I hear a melody from Tchaikovsky. I want to be right here. . . . So, my search is constantly how to elicit in collaboration with the dance new music from new composers.
>
> The other aspect about music concerns using pre-recorded sound. . . . I feel that one of the great challenges of our existence is to see how we are truly alive through immediacy before the day we die. . . . That word "immediacy" means nothing in the middle. And so, the use of any machine in relation to an art experience I think is false. I feel that in the same way that you want the livingness of the human body on the stage, you have to have the livingness of musical performance. And so, I have never performed to taped music in my life.

Hawkins' most important artistic collaborator was Polish-American composer Lucia Dlugoszewski. For many of the Hawkins-Dlugoszewski collaborations, Hawkins first created the dance and then Dlugoszewski composed music as an independently coexisting theater of sound that could relate to the movement either by evoking it or momentarily demolishing it. The unique approach to their collaboration created theater in which the movement and music are seamlessly interwoven. In a 1990 interview with Dlugoszewski, she explained to me the poetry of sound with movement and the aesthetic aims of their approach:

> Erick and I both felt that the most exciting collaboration should be two equal art forms going side by side together and relating very sensitively moment by moment to one another, but still having an identity of their own.[125]

© PETER KAPLAN

Composer Lucia Dlugoszewski with her glass ladder harp, c. 1987.

Beginning in the 1950s, when Hawkins first founded his company, and through the 1960s, music scores for Hawkins dances included instrumentation ranging anywhere from Dlugoszewski playing her invention, the "timbre" piano, to a score for the one hundred percussion instruments she also invented, to Dlugoszewski's stretching the capabilities of the conventional instruments in the Hawkins Theatre Orchestra. During the early 1970s, Hawkins began to create dances for larger orchestras, including three symphonic pieces in which

---

[125] Lucia Dlugoszewski, *The Erick Hawkins Modern Dance Technique Video*, Part II. Dlugoszewski's voice on the video is taken from a 1990 video interview with Hawkins and Dlugoszewski filmed by visual artist Douglas Rosenberg.

Lucia Dlugoszewski and sculptor Ralph Dorazio with percussion instruments invented by Dlugoszewski and made by Dorazio, 1961.

both the orchestra and dancers were onstage. These included: *Classic Kite Tails* (1972), composed by David Diamond; *Dawn Dazzled Door* (1972), composed by Toru Takemitsu; and *Meditations on Orpheus* (1974), composed by Alan Hovhaness.

From the mid-1970s onward, Hawkins started to request commissioned scores that would fit the Hawkins Theatre Orchestra, which consisted of a flute/piccolo, clarinet/bass clarinet, violin, double bass, trumpet, bass trombone and percussion.[126]

In the visual designs for his dances, Hawkins was, once again, very involved in all aspects of the process. Three of his most important design collaborators were sculptor/set designer Ralph Dorazio, visual artist Ralph Lee (responsible for all of the Hawkins repertory headdresses and masks), and lighting designer Robert Engstrom. The working process

---

[126] In commissioning scores, Hawkins would first communicate his ideas to the composer, describing the theme, mood and structure he desired sometimes in a general way, sometimes in great detail. Upon receiving the score, he would often request changes if the score did not match his structural or dramatic needs.

with these artists was very much the same as with his composers: Hawkins would present his ideas either through verbal description, sketches or a creative trial-and-error process. Based upon these meetings, the designs would develop.

All Hawkins Company sets and properties are as beautifully made and sensitively finished on their back sides as they are on their front sides. Hawkins believed that the love and care that went into such detail was integral to the creative act of experiencing the completeness of Zen immediacy.

Hawkins was very concerned that the costumes support but not take away from the movement, either by being too over-powering or not carefully enough considered. Because he felt them to be such an integral part of the dance, Hawkins would always have a rehearsal version of the costumes made before choreography began. He believed that the way the costumes moved and the way the dancers moved in them was essential to the creation of the movement vocabulary. In the following list of works, where the name Tad Taggart

© MARY BLOOM

Ralph Lee building a griffin for his Mettawee River Company, 1987.

appears, or when the costumer's name is omitted, Hawkins was the costume designer. Tad Taggart was Hawkins' costume designer pseudonym. Hawkins purposely omitted his name or used the name Tad Taggart on many of his costume designs because he wanted as much attention as possible to be focused on the choreography.

In creating costumes, Hawkins would often stand before a dancer with an irregularly shaped piece of fabric, or an owl or eagle's feather he had been saving for years, or a bundle of horsehair he had found out

© PETER PAPADOPOLOUS

John Wiatt, Cori Terry, Randy Howard and Jana
Steele in Ralph Lee's beautiful headdresses for
Plains Daybreak, 1977.

West. He would look and place the items carefully against one part or
another of the dancer's body. The aesthetic demands of correct proportion, symmetry, contrast and relationship to the theme governed these
costume details as much as they did his choreography. It involved what
Dlugoszewski and Hawkins called the "suchness"of all elements.[127]

A dance work is one of the most fragile forms of art. No score, no
record exists other than that which is available through Labanotation or
the two-dimensional media of film, videotape and CD-ROM. Therefore,
the chances of long-term survival for many of these Hawkins dances is a
serious concern. An asterisk (*) denotes those dances that presently are
neither notated nor recorded on film or videotape.

[127] Dlugoszewski interview, September 1999. Dlugoszewski describes the term "suchness" as the term "thusness"
coined by French theater poet Antonin Artaud, "epiclettiing" used by James Joyce and the ineffable quality that
permeates all of Eastern Zen–inspired culture.

WORKS CHOREOGRAPHED BY ERICK HAWKINS

(Listed in chronological order according to premiere dates)

SHOWPIECE*[128]
1937
Bennington College, Bennington, Vermont
Music: Robert McBride
Dancers: Members of the Ballet Caravan

INSUBSTANTIAL PAGEANT*
1940
92nd Street Y, New York, New York
Music: Lehman Engel
Sets: Carlos Dyer
Dancer: Erick Hawkins

IN TIME OF ARMAMENT*
1941
92nd Street Y, New York, New York
Music: Hunter Johnson
Dancer: Erick Hawkins

LIBERTY TREE*
1941
92nd Street Y, New York, New York
Music: Ralph Gilbert
Set: Carlos Dyer
Dancer: Erick Hawkins
  i.   Patriot Massachusetts
  ii. Trailbreaker Kentucky
  iii. Free-Stater Kansas
  iv. Nomad Harvester California

TRICKSTER COYOTE
1941
(revived 1965 and 1983)
92nd Street Y, New York, New York
Music: Henry Cowell
Mask: James W. Harker
Dancer: Erick Hawkins

Erick Hawkins in *Insubstantial Pageant*, Bennington College, 1940.

128 * = Choreographic works neither notated nor recorded on film or videotape.

CURTAIN RAISER*
1942
92nd Street Y, New York, New York
Music: Aaron Copland
Dancer: Erick Hawkins

PRIMER FOR ACTION*
1942
92nd Street Y, New York, New York
Music: Ralph Gilbert
Set: Carlos Dyer
Dancer: Erick Hawkins

YANKEE BLUEBRITCHES*
1942
92nd Street Y, New York, New York
Music: Hunter Johnson
Set: Charlotte Trowbridge
Dancer: Erick Hawkins

THE PARTING*
1943
92nd Street Y, New York, New York
Music: Hunter Johnson
Dancers: Jean Erdman, Erick Hawkins

SATURDAY NIGHT* (or, Party Going)
1943
Sweetbriar College, Sweetbriar, Virginia
Music: Gregory Tucker
Dancers: Muriel Brenner, Erick Hawkins,
Pearl Lang

THE PILGRIM'S PROGRESS*
1944
92nd Street Y, New York, New York
Music: Wallingford Riegger
Set: Philip Stapp
Dancer: Erick Hawkins

JOHN BROWN
February 18, 1947
(revived as *God's Angry Man* 1965 and
1985)
Constitution Hall, Philadelphia,
Pennsylvania
Music: Charles Mills
Poetry: Robert Richman
Set: Isamu Noguchi
Dancer: Captain John Brown:
Erick Hawkins
Interlocutor: Anthony Mannino

STEPHEN ACROBAT*
February 26, 1947
Ziegfeld Theater, New York, New York
Music: Robert Evett
Poetry: Robert Richman
Set: Arch Lauterer and Isamu Noguchi
Dancers: Erick Hawkins,
Stuart (Gescheidt) Hodes
Interlocutor: Anthony Mannino

THE STRANGLER*
August 22, 1948
Palmer Auditorium, American Dance
Festival at Connecticut College,
New London, Connecticut
Music: Bohuslav Martinů
Poetry: Robert Fitzgerald
Set: Arch Lauterer
Dancers: Oedipus: Erick Hawkins
Sphinx: Anne Meacham
Chorus: Joseph Wiseman

openings of the (eye)*
1952
92nd Street Y, New York, New York
Music: Lucia Dlugoszewski
Set: Ralph Dorazio
Dancer: Erick Hawkins
  i. Discovery of the Minotaur
  ii. Disconsolate Chimera
  iii. Ritual of the Descent
  iv. Goat of the God
  v. Eros, the Firstborn (excerpts on film)

BRIDEGROOM OF THE MOON*
1952
92nd Street Y, New York, New York
Music: Wallingford Riegger
Set: Louise Bourgeois
Dancer: Erick Hawkins

BLACK HOUSE*
1952
92nd Street Y, New York, New York
Music: Lucia Dlugoszewski
Designs: Ralph Dorazio
Dancer: Erick Hawkins

LIVES OF FIVE OR SIX SWORDS*
1952
92nd Street Y, New York, New York
Music: Lou Harrison
Set: Ralph Dorazio
Dancer: Erick Hawkins

Erick Hawkins in *openings of the (eye)*, c. 1958.

here and now, with watchers
(excerpts on film),
November 24, 1957
Hunter (College) Playhouse, New York,
New York
Music: Lucia Dlugoszewski
Set: Ralph Dorazio
Dancers: Erick Hawkins, Nancy Lang
(choreographed on Eva Raining)
  i. THE
  ii. INSIDE WONDER OR WHALES
    (says my body of things)
  iii. (vulnerable male is)
  iv. HERE MADE OF FALLING (and
    my body)
  v. (invisible house of female)
  vi. MULTIPLICITY (or flowers)
  vii. (CLOWN IS EVERYONE'S
    ENDING)
  viii. the (effortless) now: LIKE DARLING
    (shouts my body and shouts itself
    transparent)

8 clear places*
October 8, 1960
Hunter (College) Playhouse, New York,
New York
Music: Lucia Dlugoszewski
Set: Ralph Dorazio
Dancers: Erick Hawkins, Barbara Tucker
(choreographed on Eva Raining)
  i North Star
  ii. Pine Tree
  iii. rain, rain
  iv. cloud
  v. sheen on water
  vi. inner feet of the summer fly
  vii. they moving
  viii. squash

SUDDEN SNAKE-BIRD
1960
Music: Lucia Dlugoszewski
Set: Ralph Dorazio
Dancers: Bird: Erick Hawkins; Snake: Kelly
Holt, Kenneth LaVrack

EARLY FLOATING[129]

(21 minutes)
June 30, 1961
Portland, Oregon
Music: Lucia Dlugoszewski
Set: Ralph Dorazio
Dancers: Erick Hawkins, Kelly Holt,
Kenneth LaVrack, Ruth Ravon

"When William Saroyan says, 'The surprise of art is not shock but wonder,' he has the tender side of the world in mind. *Early Floating* is a dance concerned with tenderness between people and with surprise. The music for *Early Floating* is for 'timbre piano' using four different complex sonorities or 'curtains of timbre,' based on consonant or 'white' intervals."[130]

SPRING AZURE*

1963
Hunter (College) Playhouse, New York,
New York
Music: Lucia Dlugoszewski
Set: Ralph Dorazio
Dancers: Erick Hawkins, Kelly Holt,
Albert Reid

CANTILEVER*[131]

(16 minutes)
Dedicated to American architect
Frederick Kiesler
June 30, 1963 (piano score)
Théâtre Recamier, Théâtre des Nations
Festival, Paris, France
U.S. Premiere: (orchestral score)
August 13, 1964
Palmer Auditorium, American Dance
Festival at Connecticut College,
New London, Connecticut
Music: Lucia Dlugoszewski
Set: Ralph Dorazio
Lights: Thomas Skelton
Dancers: Pauline DeGroot, Erick Hawkins,
Nancy Meehan, Kelly Holt

"This is a New York dance, or it could be a San Francisco dance when you climb to the top of a brand new building and look out for miles. It is dedicated to the love of American architects who are building the exciting new American cities. In the music for *Cantilever* each dance gesture creates a tiny length of time that becomes a separate little piece of music resting on a consonant or 'eradiant' ground that unifies the work. At one point these little pieces take the form of isolated melodies, ending with only the thick eradiant ground of solid sound."[132]

TO EVERYBODY OUT THERE*

August 13, 1964
Palmer Auditorium, American Dance
Festival at Connecticut College,
New London, Connecticut
Music: Lucia Dlugoszewski
Set: Ralph Dorazio
Dancers: Pauline DeGroot, Erick Hawkins,
Beverly Hirschfeld, Kelly Holt, Nancy Meehan, Marilyn Patton, James Tyler,
Ellen Marshall
  i. Clown
  ii. Lovers
  iii. Friends
  iv. Woman Alone
  v. Man Alone

GEOGRAPHY OF NOON*

(excerpts on film)
August 13, 1964
Palmer Auditorium, American Dance
Festival at Connecticut College,
New London, Connecticut
New York Premiere: September 19, 1965
(with dancers Erick Hawkins, Ellen Marshall,
Dena Medole and James Tyler)
Music: Lucia Dlugoszewski
(performed onstage by Dlugoszewski)
Set: Ralph Dorazio
Dancers: Eastern Tailed Blue: Nancy
Meehan; Cloudless Sulphur: James Tyler

---

[129] *Early Floating* was choreographed as a companion piece to *8 clear places*.

[130] Program note, February 25 and 26, 1966, Hunter (College) Playhouse, New York, New York.

[131] *Cantilever* was revised as a six-person dance in February 1966, with an expanded score for eight instruments. Other versions of the dance were performed throughout the 1960s and early 1970s for concerts and lecture-demonstrations. The expanded score and some of the same movement vocabulary were later used for the twelve-person dance *Cantilever II* (1988).

[132] Program note, February 25 and 26, 1966, Hunter (College) Playhouse, New York, New York.

(choreographed on Kelly Holt); Spring
Azure: Pauline DeGroot; Variegated
Fritillary: Erick Hawkins

LORDS OF PERSIA
(16 minutes)
Commissioned by the American Dance
Festival, July 31, 1965
Palmer Auditorium, American Dance
Festival at Connecticut College,
New London, Connecticut
New York Premiere: September 19, 1965,
Hunter (College) Playhouse
Music: Lucia Dlugoszewski
Set (and sticks): Ralph Dorazio
Painting: Raymond Parker
Costumes: Ruth Sobotka (revised by
Ralph Lee)
Dancers: Erick Hawkins, Kelly Holt, Rod
Rodgers, James Tyler

"Polo was first played in Persia. This is a
dance about polo, played in three periods.
The Persian poet Firdausi wrote, 'His
Majesty, who is an excellent judge of
mankind, uses the sport of polo as a latent
means of discovering a person's merit. Polo
tests the value of a man and strengthens the
bonds of friendship.'"[133]

NAKED LEOPARD*
September 19, 1965
Hunter (College) Playhouse, New York,
New York
Music: Zoltán Kodály (solo for cello)
Designs: Ralph Dorazio
Dancer: Erick Hawkins

"Inside everyone is an animal innocence that
sometimes takes a lifetime to
recognize and cherish."[134]

DAZZLE ON A KNIFE'S EDGE*
February 25, 1966
Hunter (College) Playhouse, New York,
New York
Music: Lucia Dlugoszewski
Dancers: Erick Hawkins, Beverly Hirschfeld,
Kelly Holt, Dena Madole, Barbara Roan,

Rod Rodgers, Penelope Shaw, James Tyler
"Fun is the edge, the uncluttered moment,
passion without confusion."[135]

TIGHTROPE*
(excerpts on film)
November 14, 1968
Brooklyn Academy of Music, Brooklyn,
New York
Music: Lucia Dlugoszewski
Designs: Tad Taggart
Lighting: Chenault Spence
Dancers: First Everyone: Dena Madole;
Second Everyone: Kelly Holt
Angel: Robert Yohn
First Celestial: Beverly Brown
Second Celestial: Kay Gilbert
Third Celestial: Carol Ann Turoff

BLACK LAKE
(40 minutes)
October 20, 1969
Theater of the Riverside Church,
New York, New York
Music: Lucia Dlugoszewski
Set: Ralph Dorazio
Costumes: Tad Taggart
Lighting: Chenault Spence
Dancers: Sun: Beverly Brown
Night People: Kay Gilbert, Erick Hawkins,
Natalie Richman
Nightbirds: Erick Hawkins, Robert Yohn
Moon & Clouds: Beverly Brown, Nancy
Meehan, Natalie Richman
Comet: Kay Gilbert
Thunder: Erick Hawkins
Lightning: Beverly Brown
Bears: Kay Gilbert, Robert Yohn
Milky Way: Beverly Brown, Kay Gilbert,
Erick Hawkins, Nancy Meehan, Natalie
Richman, Robert Yohn

OF LOVE*
March 9, 1971
ANTA Theater, New York, New York
Music: Lucia Dlugoszewski
Set: Helen Frankenthaler
Lighting: Robert Engstrom
Dancers: Beverly Brown, Carol Conway,

[133] Ibid.
[134] Ibid.
[135] Ibid.

Bill Groves, Erick Hawkins, Nada Reagan,
Lillo Way, Robert Yohn

ANGELS OF THE INMOST HEAVEN
October 11, 1971
Washington, D.C.
New York Premiere: October 26, 1972,
ANTA Theater
Music: Lucia Dlugoszewski
Costumes: Erick Hawkins
Lighting: Robert Engstrom
Dancers: Beverly Brown, Carol Conway,
Erick Hawkins, Nada Reagan, Natalie
Richman, Robert Yohn

CLASSIC KITE TAILS
(21 minutes)
July 11, 1972
Meadowbrook Festival, Detroit, Michigan
New York Premiere: October 26, 1972,
ANTA Theater
Music: David Diamond (*Rounds for String
Orchestra*) for full string orchestra
Set: Stanley Boxer
Lighting: Robert Engstrom
Dancers: Beverly Brown, Carol Conway,
Erick Hawkins, Nada Reagan, Natalie
Richman, Lillo Way, Robert Yohn

DAWN DAZZLED DOOR
(17 minutes)
July 1972
Meadowbrook Festival, Detroit, Michigan
New York Premiere: October 26, 1972,
ANTA Theater
Music: Toru Takemitsu (*Dorian Horizon*)
for full symphony orchestra
Set: Ralph Dorazio
Lighting: Robert Engstrom
Dancers: Beverly Brown, Carol Conway,
Erick Hawkins, Natalie Richman, Lillo Way,
Robert Yohn

GREEK DREAMS, WITH FLUTE
September 7, 1973
Solomon R. Guggenheim Museum,
New York, New York
Music: Claude Debussy, Ohama, Alan
Hovhaness, Matsudiara, Jolivet, Edgard
Varèse: for flute
Set: Ralph Dorazio
Lighting: Robert Engstrom
Dancers:
  i. nymph of the grass & meadow: Cathy
     Ward
  ii. gymnopaidia & strophe of gift bringers:
      Carol Conway, Nada Reagan, Natalie
      Richman, Robert Yohn
  iii. year—daimon: Erick Hawkins
  iv. chorus of daughters of Okeanos:

Beverly Brown, Carol Conway, Nathalie Richman, Nada Reagan Diachenko, Bob Yohn and
Erick Hawkins in *Greek Dreams, with Flute*, c. 1973.

© DAVID GEOFF

Beverly Brown, Carol Conway,
Nada Reagan, Natalie Richman;
Plato's halves are part of whole:
Cathy Ward, Robert Yohn
v. satyr play: Ensemble

MEDITATIONS ON ORPHEUS*
(excerpts on film)
July 19, 1974
Kennedy Center, Washington, D.C.
New York Premiere: September 11, 1975,
Carnegie Hall
Music: Alan Hovhaness, for full symphony
orchestra
Set: Ray Sais
Costumes: Raya
Lighting: Robert Engstrom
Dancers: Carol Conway, Erick Hawkins,
Arlene Kennedy, Alan Lynes, Nada Reagan,
Natalie Richman, Kevin Tobiason,
Cathy Ward

HURRAH!
(17 minutes)
July 5, 1975
Blossom Music Center (with the Cleveland
Orchestra), Cleveland, Ohio
New York Premiere: September 11, 1975,
Carnegie Hall
Music: Virgil Thomson (*Symphony No. 2
in C Major*)
Set: Ralph Dorazio
Costumes: Nancy Cope
Lighting: Robert Engstrom
Dancers: Erick Hawkins, Victor Lucas, Alan
Lynes, Kristin Peterson, Nada Reagan,
Natalie Richman, Cathy Ward, Robert Yohn

DEATH IS THE HUNTER
(14 minutes) notation score exists
September 11, 1975
Carnegie Hall
Music: Wallingford Riegger (*Study in
Sonority*)
Masks and Set: Ralph Lee
Costumes: Willa Kim (for Dramatis
Personae)
Lighting: Robert Engstrom
Dancers: Death: Erick Hawkins; Stage
Shadow: Kevin Tobiason; Dramatis
Personae: Alan Lynes, Nada Reagan,
Natalie Richman, Cathy Ward,
John Wiatt, Robert Yohn

PARSON WEEMS AND THE CHERRY TREE, ETC . . .
November 1, 1976
(for the United States Bicentennial)
University of Massachusetts, Amherst,
Massachusetts
Music: Virgil Thomson
Set: Ralph Dorazio, Ray Sais
Masks: Ralph Lee
Lighting: Robert Engstrom
Dancers: Clown: Erick Hawkins; George
Washington: Robert Yohn; Martha
Washington: Nada Reagan; Parson Weems:
John Wiatt; Molly Pitcher: Natalie Richman;
Flag: Cathy Ward

PLAINS DAYBREAK
(31 minutes)
April 19, 1979
Cincinnati, Ohio
Music: Alan Hovhaness
Set: Ralph Dorazio
Masks: Ralph Lee
Lighting: Robert Engstrom
Dancers: First Man: Erick Hawkins;
Raccoon: Laura Pettibone; Snake: Cori Terry;
Buffalo: Douglas Andresen; Fish: Cynthia
Reynolds; Antelope: Jesse Duranceau;
Coyote: Randy Howard; Porcupine: Craig
Nazor; Hawk: Cathy Ward

Erick Hawkins and Cynthia Reynolds in
Death Is the Hunter, 1986.

Randy Howard, Gloria McLean, Mark Wisniewski, Cathy Ward (partially visible), Daniel Tai, Laura Pettibone, James Reedy and Cynthia Reynolds in *Summer Clouds People*, c. 1984.

AGATHLON
(21 minutes)
July 1979
Festival of Nervi, Genoa, Italy
U.S. Premiere: January 16, 1980
Whitney Museum of Art, New York,
New York
Music: Dorrance Stalvey
Set: Ralph Dorazio
Lighting: Robert Engstrom
Dancers: Douglas Andresen, Jesse Duran-
ceau, Randy Howard, Craig Nazor, Laura
Pettibone, Cynthia Reynolds, Cori Terry,
Cathy Ward

AVANTI*
(unfinished)
June 26, 1980
American Dance Festival at Duke University,
Durham, North Carolina
Music: Lucia Dlugoszewski
Lighting: Robert Engstrom
Dancers: Douglas Andresen, Jesse Duran-
ceau, Randy Howard, Craig Nazor, Laura
Pettibone, Cynthia Reynolds, Cori Terry,
Cathy Ward

HEYOKA
(17 minutes)
September 14, 1981
Alice Tully Hall, New York, New York
Music: Ross Lee Finney
Set: Ralph Dorazio
Lighting: Robert Engstrom
Dancers: Douglas Andresen, Jesse Duran-
ceau, Randy Howard, Craig Nazor, Helen
Pelton, Laura Pettibone, Cynthia Reynolds,
Cathy Ward

SUMMER CLOUDS PEOPLE
(20 minutes)
February 9, 1983
Joyce Theater, New York, New York
Music: Michio Mamiya
Set: Ralph Dorazio
Lighting: Robert Engstrom
Dancers: Douglas Andresen, Randy Howard,
Helen Pelton, Laura Pettibone, Cynthia
Reynolds, Daniel Tai, Cathy Ward, Mark
Wisniewski

TRICKSTER COYOTE
(revival)
1983
Symphony Space, New York, New York
Music: Henry Cowell
Dancers: Coyote: Randy Howard; The
People: Laura Pettibone, Cynthia Reynolds,
Daniel Tai, Mark Wisniewski

THE JOSHUA TREE
October 10, 1984
Joyce Theater, New York, New York
Music: Ross Lee Finney
Set: Ralph Dorazio
Costumes: Ray Sais
Lighting: Robert Engstrom
Dancers: Erick Hawkins, Randy Howard,
James Reedy, Daniel Tai, Mark Wisniewski

GOD'S ANGRY MAN
1985
(reconstruction of *John Brown*)
Joyce Theater, New York, New York
Music: Charles Mills

Poetry: Robert Richman
Set: Isamu Noguchi
Dancer: Captain John Brown:
Erick Hawkins

TODAY, WITH DRAGON
February 5, 1986
Alice Tully Hall, New York, New York
Music: Ge Gan-Ru
Set: Ralph Dorazio
Costumes: Patrick Elliott
Lighting: Robert Engstrom
Dancers: Erick Hawkins, Randy Howard,
Gloria McLean, Laura Pettibone, James
Reedy, Cynthia Reynolds, Daniel Tai, Cathy
Ward, Mark Wisniewski

AHAB
(commissioned for Harvard University's
350th anniversary)
September 4, 1986
Hasty Pudding Theatre, Cambridge,
Massachusetts
Music: Ross Lee Finney

Randy Howard, James Reedy, Mark Wisniewski and Erick Hawkins in *The Joshua Tree*, c. 1984.

Brenda Connors, Kathy Ortiz, Joseph Mills (partially visible), Gloria McLean and Michael Moses in *Killer of Enemies*, 1991.

Text: Herman Melville
Set: Ralph Dorazio
Masks: Ralph Lee
Lighting: Robert Engstrom
Dancers: Captain Ahab: Erick Hawkins; First Mate: Randy Howard; The Harpooners: Michael Moses, James Reedy, Daniel Tai; Queequeg: Michael Moses; Ishmael/Interlocutor: Michael Butler

GOD THE REVELLER
October 28, 1987
The John F. Kennedy Center,
Washington, D.C.
Music: Alan Hovhaness
Set: Ralph Dorazio
Design Assistant: Timothy McMinn
Lighting: Robert Engstrom
Dancers: Katherine Duke, Randy Howard, Gloria McLean, Michael Moses, Laura Pettibone, James Reedy, Cynthia Reynolds, Sean Russo, Daniel Tai, Mariko Tanabe, Mark Wisniewski

CANTILEVER II
(16 minutes)
December 6, 1988
Joyce Theater, New York, New York
Music: Lucia Dlugoszewski
Set: Ralph Dorazio
Lighting: Robert Engstrom
Dancers: James Aarons, Brenda Connors, Katherine Duke, Randy Howard, Gloria McLean, Michael Moses, Laura Pettibone, James Reedy, Cynthia Reynolds, Sean Russo, Daniel Tai, Mariko Tanabe

NEW MOON
November 28, 1989
Joyce Theater, New York, New York
Music: Lou Harrison
Set: Ralph Dorazio
Costumes: Erick Hawkins
Lighting: Robert Engstrom
Dancers: Douglas Andresen, Renata Celichowska, Brenda Connors, Katherine Duke, Gloria McLean, Michael Moses, Laura Pettibone, Christopher Potts, Cynthia Reynolds, Frank Roth, Sean Russo, Catherine Tharin

KILLER OF ENEMIES:
THE DIVINE HERO
(48 minutes)
March 26, 1991
Joyce Theater, New York, New York
Music: Alan Hovhaness
Set: Ralph Dorazio
Headdresses: Ralph Lee
Lighting: Robert Engstrom
Interlocutors: Robert Engstrom,
Jeffrey Kensmoe
Dancers: Old Man: Erick Hawkins; Killer of
Enemies: Michael Moses; Changing Woman:
Gloria McLean; Spider Woman: Cynthia
Reynolds; Big Giant: Othello Johns; Monster
Eagle: Douglas Andresen; Monster Owl:
Laura Pettibone; Big Fly: Joseph Mills;
Little Wind: Catherine Tharin; Holy People:
Renata Celichowska, Brenda Connors,
Kathy Ortiz, Catherine Tharin

INTENSITIES OF WIND & SPACE
(11 minutes)
March 27, 1991
Joyce Theater, New York, New York
Music: Katsuhisa Hattori
Set: Ralph Dorazio
Lighting: Robert Engstrom

Dancers: Douglas Anderesen, Brenda
Connors, Othello Johns, Gloria McLean,
Joseph Mills, Michael Moses, Laura
Pettibone, Cynthia Reynolds, Frank Roth,
Catherine Tharin

EACH TIME YOU CARRY ME
THIS WAY
February 23, 1993
Joyce Theater, New York, New York
Music: Lucia Dlugoszewski
Lighting: Robert Engstrom
Dancers: Coleen McIntosh Blacklock,
Othello Johns, Joseph McClintock, Gloria
McLean, Tim McMinn, Joseph Mills, Kathy
Ortiz, Christopher Potts, Brian Simmerson,
Mariko Tanabe, Catherine Tharin

MANY THANKS
January 25, 1994
Joyce Theater, New York, New York
Music: Performed in silence on premiere,
later scored by Lucia Dlugoszewski
Lighting: Robert Engstrom
Dancers: Coleen McIntosh Blacklock, Joseph
Mills, Michael Moses, Kathy Ortiz,
Christopher Potts, Brian Simmerson, Mariko
Tanabe, Catherine Tharin

Joseph Mills and Catherine Tharin in *Intensities of Space & Wind*, 1991.

"The natural state of man's mind is delight" — Toju Nakae. Erick Hawkins in "Clown Is Everyone's Ending" from *here and now, with watchers*, c. 1960.

LABANOTATION

ABOUT THE NOTATION PROCESS

The Labanotation examples in this book were notated in private sessions between the notator, Ilene Fox, and the Project Director, Renata Celichowska. Fox had studied at the Hawkins studio and had some familiarity with the principles. She also spent time watching classes during the project period.

During the private sessions, Fox and Celichowska looked at footage from the documentary, discussed in depth the examples that were selected for notation, performed them and Fox did preliminary notation. This notation was refined before the next meeting, at which time any questions were answered.

After the examples were completed, Valarie Williams Mockabee (faculty, The Ohio State University Dance Department) learned the exercises from the notation and showed the results to Celichowska and Cynthia Reynolds. Further changes were made based on their feedback. Celichowska said of this demonstration:

> I watched while the Hawkins form magically emerged from the page into a living, breathing movement. The accuracy and depth of the reader's understanding of the movement gave me a whole new appreciation of dance notation and its valuable contribution in preserving Erick's work.

The final version of the examples were then proofread by Mockabee, Ray Cook and the Dance Notation Bureau notation staff: Sandra Aberkalns, Robin Hoffman and Leslie Rotman. Final corrections were made.

READING LABANOTATION

Many of the exercises in this book have been recorded in Labanotation. Labanotation captures all the detail of the movement in a way that makes it easy to study and perform. Here are some Labanotation basics to get you started.

Each Labanotation symbol gives four pieces of information:

1.   Direction of the movement is indicated by the shape of the symbol. (See diagram.)

2.   The level of a movement is shown by the shading of the symbol; diagonal strokes for high, a dot for middle, and blackened for low.

   forward high   forward middle   forward low

3.   The part of the body that is moving is indicated by the column on the staff in which the symbol is placed. A Labanotation staff represents the human body; the center line of the staff divides the left side of the body from the right. Symbols to the left of the center line refer to the left-hand side of the body, symbols to the right of the center line to the right-hand side of the body.

Some body parts must be identified by a symbol, for example:

C = the head   = the face   = the hands   = the front of the left shoulder

4.   Duration of the movement is shown by the length of the symbol. The staff is read from the bottom up, moving ahead in time. The tick marks on the center line divide the time into counts and the horizontal lines correspond with the bar lines in the music. Movements written on the same horizontal line occur simultaneously; movements written one above another occur sequentially. Measure numbers and dancers' counts appear to the left of the staff.

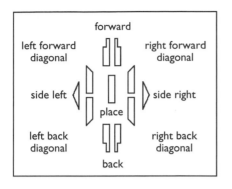

Direction Symbols

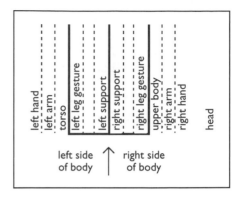

The Staff

GLOSSARY

Below are some notation usages specific to the examples in this book.

Initiate bow. A body part sign placed inside the bow tells you which part of the body starts the movement. In the example below, the torso tilts forward high, folded one degree. The movement begins in the pelvis.

Heel end of the foot. It is used in the example below to show that the fingers are grabbing the heel end of the foot.

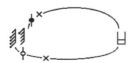

The walk of the foot. The walk of the foot is the little toe side of the ball of the foot. It is not the side of the foot, it is the ball, but the whole ball is not contacting the floor.

The knees are touching, but the touch does not need to be rigidly held. Used in the figure 8 exercise, the touch can adjust or release slightly as the legs move.

 The "pads" (palm side) of the last segment of the fingers.

 When the legs are turned out, they should rotate, not twist. Turn out as much as possible without twisting.

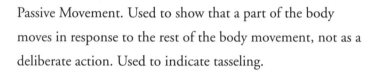 Passive Movement. Used to show that a part of the body moves in response to the rest of the body movement, not as a deliberate action. Used to indicate tasseling.

For further study of Labanotation contact Princeton Book Company, Publishers, P.O. Box 831, Hightstown, NJ 08520 (Tel. 609-426-0602; Fax 609-426-1344; email: pbc@dancehorizons.com) and ask for their catalog.

RECOMMENDED READING

The following is a compilation of books frequently recommended by Erick Hawkins.

Benoit, Hubert. *The Supreme Doctrine*, Inner Traditions International, Ltd., New York, 1984.

Blyth, R. H. Four volumes: *Autumn Winter, Eastern Culture, Spring, Summer Autumn.*

_____. *Zen in English Literature and Oriental Classics,* Book East, Portland, 1942.

Campbell, Joseph. Hawkins recommended all Campbell, including:

_____. *Hero with a Thousand Faces,* Pantheon, New York, 1949.

_____. *The Inner Reaches of Outer Space: Metaphor as Myth and as Religion*, A. Van Der Marck Eds., New York, 1986.

_____. *The Mythic Image,* Princeton University Press, Princeton, 1974.

_____. *Occidental Mythology,* Penguin Books, New York, 1976.

Fowlie, Wallace. *Age of Surrealism,* Swallow Press, New York, 1950.

Herrigel, Eugen. *Zen in the Art of Archery,* New York, Pantheon Books, 1953.

Kadensho, Ze-Ami. *Noh Drama,* translated by Shuishi Sakurai, Shuseki Hayashi, Rokuro Satoi, Bin Miyai. Foundation of Sumiya-Shinobe Scholarship, Doshisha University, Kyoto, 1963.

Krishnamurti, Jiddu. (Hawkins recommended all Krishnamurti).

_____. *Beyond Violence,* Harper & Row, New York, 1973.

_____. *Commentaries on Living,* Theosophical Publishing House, Wheaton, 1967.

_____. *Education and the Significance of Life,* Harper, New York, 1953.

_____. *The First and Last Freedom,* Harper, New York, 1954.

_____. *Freedom from the Known,* Harper & Row, New York, 1969.

_____. *From Darkness to Light: Poems and Parables,* Harper & Row, San Francisco, 1980.

_____. *The Impossible Question,* Penguin Books, New York, 1991.

_____. *The Only Revolution,* Harper & Row, New York, 1970.

Marcuse, Hubert. *Eros & Civilization,* Beacon Press, Boston, 1966.

Maritain, Jacques. (Hawkins recommended many Maritain).

_____. *Art and Poetry,* Philosophical Library, New York, 1943.

_____. *Creative Intuition in Art and Poetry.*

_____. *The Responsibility of the Artist,* Gordian Press, New York, 1972.

_____. *Science and Wisdom,* Scribner, New York, 1940.

Northrop, F. S. C. *The Logic of the Sciences and the Humanities,* Meridian Books, New York, 1959.

_____. *The Meeting of East and West,* The Macmillan Company, New York, 1946.

_____ and Luckow, Filmer Stuart. *Man, Nature and God,* Simon & Schuster, New York, 1962.

Rochlein, Harvey. *Notes on Contemporary American Dance,* University Extension Press, Baltimore, 1964.

Suzuki, Daisetz Teitaro. *Zen and Japanese Culture,* Princeton University Press, Princeton, 1970.

Suzuki, Shunryu. *Zen Mind, Beginner's Mind,* Weatherhill, New York, 1970.

Watts, Alan. *Nature, Man and Woman,* Pantheon, New York, 1958.

_____. *The Way of Zen,* Vintage Books, New York, 1989.

BIBLIOGRAPHY

Brown, Beverly. "Training to Dance with Erick Hawkins," *Five Essays on the Dance of Erick Hawkins,* Foundation for Modern Dance, New York, 1977.

Chujoy, Anatole. *The New York City Ballet: The First Twenty Years,* Da Capo Press, New York, 1982.

Cohen, Selma Jeanne. *The Modern Dance: Seven Statements of Belief,* Wesleyan University Press, Middletown, CT, 1966.

Dowd, Irene. *Taking Root to Fly,* Contact Editions, Northampton, MA, 1990.

Franklin, Eric. *Dance Imagery for Technique and Performance,* Human Kinetics, Champaign, IL, 1996.

_____. *Dynamic Alignment Through Imagery,* Human Kinetics, Champaign, IL, 1996.

Hawkins, Erick. *The Body Is a Clear Place,* Princeton Book Company, Publishers, Princeton, 1992.

Humphrey, Doris. *The Art of Making Dances,* Grove Press Inc., New York, 1959; reprinted by Princeton Book Company, Publishers, Princeton.

Norton, M. L. Gordon. *Five Essays on the Dance of Erick Hawkins,* Sheldon Soffer Management, New York, 1980.

Sweigard, Lulu E., Ph.D. *Human Movement Potential: Its Ideokinetic Facilitation,* Harper & Row, New York, 1974.

Todd, Mabel E. *The Thinking Body,* Paul B. Hoeber, Inc., New York, 1937; reprinted by Princeton Book Company, Publishers, Princeton.

VIDEOGRAPHY

Erick Hawkins, America, distributed by Princeton Book Company, Publishers, 1992.

The Erick Hawkins Modern Dance Technique, Part I, distributed by Princeton Book Company Publishers, 2000.

The Erick Hawkins Modern Dance Technique, Part II, distributed by Princeton Book Company Publishers, 2000.

INDEX

undercurves, 34–35
vertical axis, 36–37
voluntary movement patterns, 17

Ward, Cathy, 110, 113, 124
weight shifting, 32–34

Why Does a Man Dance?, xxv
winged arm, 67

Yankee Bluebritches, 150

Zen Buddhism, xix